THE WINNING EDGE IN SELLING

THE WINNING EDGE
IN SELLING

Robert E. Eastman

Prentice-Hall, Inc.
Englewood Cliffs, NJ

Prentice-Hall International, Inc., *London*
Prentice-Hall of Australia, Pty. Ltd., *Sydney*
Prentice-Hall Canada, Inc., *Toronto*
Prentice-Hall of India Private Ltd., *New Delhi*
Prentice-Hall of Japan, Inc., *Tokyo*
Prentice-Hall of Southeast Asia Pte. Ltd., *Singapore*
Whitehall Books, Ltd., *Wellington, New Zealand*
Editora Prentice-Hall do Brasil, Ltda., *Rio de Janeiro*

Library of Congress Cataloging in Publication Data
Eastman, Robert E.
  The winning edge in selling.
  Includes index.
  1. Selling—Psychological aspects. I. Title.
HF5438.8.P75E17   1983   658.8′5   83-11134

ISBN 0-13-960989-X

Printed in the United States of America

To Spence and Bobby,
my very close friends, my sons.

FOREWORD

The first time I met Bob Eastman was in 1959. Eastman had just founded a fledgling national sales representative firm to sell time for radio stations. Eastman was already legendary for his unique charisma and success in sales and sales management. Eastman was credited as the single major force in catapulting another radio rep company from relative obscurity to a shut out number one ranking in the field.

The Eastman approach set the standard in the broadcast sales industry. Selling time for radio-TV stations is a most complex and competitive intangible sale. Almost the pure "intangible sale." Eastman's sales direction within his own firm quickly spearheaded its drive from last place (35th) to the top five in its field in less than five years. In retrospect, an astounding feat when all competitive and economic factors are taken into account.

In that I was privileged to work directly for and with Bob Eastman for 15 years—it's "duck soup" for me to share with you the startling success that comes from following the Eastman approach in the Winning Edge. His sales magic is a simple combination of planning, knowledge, attitude and perseverance. Oh, yes—add hard work and practice.

I was just one of thousands of reluctant sales folks who got infected by Bob Eastman's communicable disease of "enthusiasm plus knowledge equals more sales." *The Winning Edge in Selling* is based on solid, pragmatic, "it works" theories. Eastman taught us to welcome rejection, fear, and problems as valuable learning experiences. He said, "they all build mental muscle."

The broadcast industry is liberally sprinkled with top executives who once worked for Bob Eastman—at NBC, ABC, Blair, and the firm he personally founded. He had a knack for hiring the maximum-achiever-type of person. Eastman always led by example—he set the pace—visible in victory or defeat.

7

Bob Eastman has been acknowledged as the most effective, persuasive, and greatest broadcast salesperson in the industry's 60-year history. Nobody debates the title—just the degree of greatness.

I genuinely treasure what Bob Eastman taught me about how the Winning Edge technique usually does tip the scale to bigger sales successes. However, to succeed with the Eastman Winning Edge you must go all the way in sticking to the basics—there are no halfway measures—no fast bucks—no quick fixes and no instant sales training miracles built in.

As Jack Nicklaus said in one of his books on how to succeed in golf, "if you don't have the discipline just to keep your head down, read no further, you'll never be a successful golfer." Bob Eastman shares with you the how-to, what-to, and why-do concepts that make up this Winning Edge in Selling. He gives you the road map to successful selling.

—Frank Boyle
Chairman and Chief Executive Officer
Eastman Radio, Inc.

WHAT THIS BOOK OFFERS YOU

Here is an exciting new arsenal of winning selling methods, tested and proven to provide you with ways to tip the balance in your favor more often and expand your earnings to ever-growing new highs.

This book brings you ideas, concepts, and techniques that have been tremendously valuable for me personally and for the many superb salespeople with whom I have been associated. It goes beyond the sales basics. *The Winning Edge in Selling* comprises these extraordinary success techniques:

- *Nuances.* Subtle ideas that give you a big edge.
- *Simple procedures.* Overlooked by most of your competitors.
- *Specific devices.* Applied to attain advantages for you.
- *Concepts.* To clarify and speed the means to reach your business goals and your personal financial growth.

Even though we are dealing in the somewhat intangible area of thought processes, let me assure you we are not talking theory. These unique concepts have been tested and applied abundantly. They work. Many millions of dollars of sales commissions have been and currently are being generated with these methods. Several former associates of mine attribute much of their wealth to the application of these sound practices.

Frank B. drives a Rolls Royce—deserves it—and could afford two. Many of his valuable leadership secrets are found in the pages of this book.

Charlie C. has built a six-figure income, plus extensive equity and important executive responsibility from a foundation of certain key winning sales practices delineated in this book.

9

Bob D. tipped the balance in his favor, using nuances you'll read about, to acquire his company with nothing out of his pocket.

My younger son, Bob II, has parlayed these winning sales concepts into a growing retail chain. Recently he turned down two-and-a-half million dollars for his business.

Grand success emanates from an insatiable hunger fed by an abundant talent. The nourishment offered in these pages is readily assimilated. These successful selling techniques give you sales methods you can apply immediately. You'll enjoy using these ideas. About many you'll say, "I wonder why I never heard of that before." All have a track record of selling something to somebody.

You may disagree with certain concepts. A few are quite unorthodox. You've heard and read all the orthodox elements of selling many times. If you believe in zigging when the competition zags, you'll welcome our unorthodox techniques.

In my sales company we nurtured the thought: "Everything we're doing is wrong. Yes, *everything*—because tomorrow we'll find ways to do it all better." That's what *The Winning Edge in Selling* is about: Doing it better, and banking the commissions that came from doing a better job.

- What *you* are and what *you* do is basic. We demonstrate numerous methods to enable your personal product— your **Extra Charisma**—to accelerate your sales.

- **Creative Selling** follows—with potent ideas you will want to start applying immediately.

- Then we spotlight new **Persuasive Presentation** techniques, with a variety of ideas to dramatize your product values.

- **Perceptive Prospecting** methods aim you on target without the often-encountered wheel-spinning.

- The pen is still a sword, and we'll show you many new ways to **Win With Your Pen.**

- **Create Attitudes** that enable you to build your winning edge by adroitly molding people. It's exciting.

- **Establish Your Individual Trademark**—it gives you a

system to help make you a more unique person with a stronger selling base to build from.

- **The Power of Positiveness** that follows is a winning method with interesting and unusual money-making concepts.

- Closing, the goal of all selling, is treated as **Creative Closing.** It provides you with some different slants on ways to get to the order earlier and more frequently.

These overt and subtle qualities are mostly quite simple. Yet simplicity is not necessarily commonplace. The paper clip is most simple. Its origin is unique.

One of the country's top salespeople, Bob E. (not me!), a key executive of a major corporation, scanned these concepts on a flight from New York to Chicago. He told me, "I stole one of your ideas and landed a big sale." Another dynamic sales executive, Stan C., wrote, "I've been selling for over thirty years—I'm really surprised to realize that several of your ideas never occurred to me before."

You will find this book considerably different from any other book on selling. The focus is on numerous subtleties that have been left largely unexpressed in literature on selling. You will acquire new, valuable techniques to expand your productivity. New ideas on common selling techniques will make them more useful for you. Over and over you will find yourself saying, "Why hasn't anyone suggested this before?"

Most important, your study and application of this book's contents will bring you substantial *income growth, personal satisfaction, and competitive advantage.*

Robert E. Eastman

CONTENTS

THE WINNING EDGE IN SELLING

1 UTILIZE THE WINNING EDGE OF EXTRA CHARISMA IN YOUR SELLING TECHNIQUES

- Define *you* as the product
- Mold your personal qualities into winning power
- Use your basic talents more effectively

THE SIX STEPS
TO A NEW CHARISMATIC YOU

1. Cultivate your personal banner
2. Build an eloquence in your style
3. Adjust your six-way voice mechanism
4. Generate essential self-esteem
5. Strengthen your sales vocabulary with these seven ideas
6. Create the luster of luck

To me the most exciting thing in the world is a truly superb salesperson. I tingle all over when I meet a real winner. That person is the champ!

My open admiration, when I observe this rare epitome of selling competence, is tempered with a strong feel of humility. It is an emotional experience for me. Nothing turns me on like the sincere, competent, professional salesperson. Without exception they all possess a high level of that unique quality known as charisma, which is vastly different from "personality."

Webster's New Collegiate Dictionary defines charisma:

- An extraordinary power . . .
- A personal magic of leadership . . .
- A special magnetic charm . . .

It is my privilege to know many of America's leading executives. To a person they radiate the qualities of potent salesmanship, including the power, the magic, and the magnetism of their highly developed personal charisma.

Let's delineate your charismatic opportunities and demonstrate specific ways for you to expand this vital aspect of your winning edge.

1. CULTIVATE YOUR PERSONAL BANNER

Remember, no matter what you sell, *you are the product.* It's you that makes the difference.

Ten basic factors to cultivate your personal banner:

1. Your face
2. Your eyes
3. Your eloquence
4. Your voice
5. Your enthusiasm
6. Your gestures
7. Your empathy

8. Your attire
9. Your listening
10. Your confidence

You are the product.

A constructive program to follow is to reexamine yourself periodically on the ten basic factors.

Think About Your Face

How do you think *your face* appears through the eyes of prospects and customers? Shrewd? Lackadaisical? Domineering? Sympathetic? Cheerful? Sincere? Alert? Tired? There are at least a hundred different reactions, positive and negative, that your face may be signalling across the desk.

- Is that important?
- Is it worth thinking about?
- Is it worth doing something about?

My friend Charlie C., a marvelously charismatic salesperson and very successful in advertising, told me, "I feel that the face is the most revealing thing about a person, and most people don't think about it enough."

Think about it.

Use the mirror, study your expressions. Actors do. Every salesperson is an actor, on stage in the customer's office.

Ask your spouse or a confidant how your face comes across. Unusual thought?

Some may spout old clichés: "I am what I am," or "You can't teach an old dog new tricks," or "You can't make a silk purse out of a sow's ear." All negatives. It's *your* face. It's undoubtedly a fine face. But like everything else, it is subject to improvement, and improving it is a vital part of expanding your charisma—and your sales.

One key executive I know considered himself "not the morning type." He was content to appear impassively bored until at least 10:00 a.m. Later he learned that he could, via exercise, the cold shower, and the mirror, manage to come on stage at 8:30 a.m. with a good face. He was a far better and richer man for the effort.

Eyes That Win

Your eyes are more than just a part of your face. Every emotion shows in the eyes. You might consider that eyes are blue or brown or maybe green or gray. Observe people's eyes more closely and you find a subtle spectrum of innumerable shadings. But the color's not important; it's the *expression* that counts.

The expression in your eyes is a sales tool. You know that. You've seen some sulky-eyed people who considered themselves selling superstars. And you've observed flashing eyes with no brains behind them. *Responsive* eyes react to the mood of the customer.

- Eyes show confidence
- Eyes wheedle reaction
- Eyes convey shrewdness (for a shrewd, beneficial idea)
- Eyes show amazement

Warm eyes used skillfully can often thaw a cold prospect.

Eloquence Puts Color in Selling

Your eloquence is the ability to fit the right words into your presentation. I feel strongly that they must be *your* words, tailored to need, mood, and reactions of the customer, not someone else's words memorized—the canned pitch.

You give a great deal of advance thought to the right words. You avoid negative words. You practice good language and clear diction because it compliments your client far more than slang, slurring, and mumbles of "and-uh-ah-but-mmm." Eloquence is not pompous—it is clear and incisive and moves more directly to the close.

Sincere eloquence is an easy area for improvement of your charisma and sales gains.

Talk Convincingly

Your voice is vital and highly malleable. It can augment your winning edge. As a prime sales tool, the steps you take to improve your voice and its use are a valuable investment.

This factor of voice, as an element of your personal product is so important that I am going to give it more specific treatment later in this chapter.

Enthusiasm Adds Vitality and Zing

Enthusiasm is a major part of your charismatic capital. Despite the fact that enthusiasm has almost become a cliché in sales jargon, it is still in very short supply. You will benefit greatly by constantly re-inventorying your enthusiasm and the manner in which you use it. Dr. Norman Vincent Peale wrote an entire book on the subject: *Enthusiasm Makes the Difference.* It does! Not too many people radiate sincere, meaningful, response-evoking enthusiasm.

My former associate, Bill B., is an ardent disciple of enthusiasm. He has his sales reps literally jumping with enthusiasm.

Enthusiasm has various shadings:

- Soft and subtle
- Loud and buoyant
- Direct and sincere

. . . But always with a gleam in your eye, excitement in your voice, eloquence in your words, and an inviting expression on your face that says, "Come on, share it, it's fun!"

Your Staging Requires Gestures That Dramatize

Your gestures are a most meaningful part of your personal product. Good gestures are essential and can usually take considerable improvement. Certainly you will want to take stock regularly of this facet of your selling.

There are negative and positive gestures. Pointing, for example, can be positive or negative, depending on how it is done. Pointing to an illustration, the prospect's product, or something relative to your presentation, is positive. A jabbing finger is offensive. A salesperson's finger pointing egotistically at him- or herself is negative.

I was making a Saturday morning tour of retail establishments with a man considering going into the retail business. We entered one store, a new nursery stock store. The owner stood with his arms folded across his chest, with a most unhospitable attitude. In the next store, a stationery store, the woman smiled, held out her palms in a welcoming gesture, and said brightly, "Hello! Say, I have something wonderful to show you! Look here!"

The retail cliché, "May I help you?" beats folded arms any day. It is a joy to see some enthusiasm for the merchandise and a welcoming gesture that leads you to it and makes you want it.

Recently my friend and neighbor, Don W., who owns and operates a most successful automobile dealership in Detroit, introduced me to his son and daughter-in-law. Don's son was going to Tampa to operate a newly acquired dealership. I asked the two of them, "What is your strategy?"

Don replied, "Sell cars!"

A simple, direct, uncomplicated response. But his eyes gleamed with enthusiasm, his arms extended in a welcoming gesture, and his body leaned forward poised for action. Then he burlesqued the cliché, "May I help you?" leaving no doubt in my mind that those words would never apply to his selling methods.

Stand in the Prospect's Shoes

Your empathy—the ability to relate to your client and to make your product fit the client's needs—is essential to your winning edge. Empathy comes easily to good salespersons. Still, it is too important to leave it off the personal checklist.

The problem is: You are constantly admonished vociferously to drive, fight, never let up, with the result that aggressiveness can diminish empathy. On the other hand, you don't want to be empathetic to a degree that you frequently concur with all the prospect's objections and walk out empty-handed and mad at yourself. Your balance of drive and empathy requires examination and frequent adjustment to be sure that you are not permitting either approach to negate sales.

Aggressiveness is really not essential in selling. Numerous sales managers and salespersons would undoubtedly disagree. Some of them, you may be sure, are one-shot performers.

Perseverance is another thing.

Clothes Do Have a Bearing

Your attire makes a difference. Wait a minute, this is not an old saw about "clothes and the person." All competent sales-persons have a feeling for the proper attire to fit their market. Nevertheless you must have observed many otherwise fine salespersons with flagrant clothing errors that detracted from their effectiveness. The clothing worn by a salesperson does have some bearing on his or her effectiveness. It has to be considered.

Yes, I've seen a man, ecstatic over the compliment about his necktie, waste half of his selling time talking about the tie—where he bought it, how his wife likes it, how well the color matches his. . . . Terrible! But it happens.

There are those who posture in front of their client as if they were selling clothes instead of their product. Somehow they retain the mistaken belief that this is part of selling them-selves! Once, only once, I guarantee you—I even heard one of my own company's salespeople brag to an underpaid buyer how much he had paid for a suit.

My friend Bill K. owns a trucking company in Ohio. He buys a lot of trucks. He told me about the man who came to sell him $100,000 worth of small trucks. The so-called sales-person was wearing a beret. A beret! Okay for selling paintings on Pont Neuf in Paris. But calling on a Cleveland businessman? Never!

Some old pros persist in using little judgment when it comes to attire. That's why I put it on the checklist of some-thing we all must think about in the process of cultivating a personal banner.

- Think about your attire as it helps you fit your market.
- The good taste of your clothes should give you confi-dence in your selling environment.
- Never get trapped into a discussion of your clothes—unless that is what you are selling! Smile, shrug, throw away the compliment, and use it as a springboard to your opening sales point.

- The wise, subtle, and appropriate utilization of attire will sharpen your selling.

Your Ears Are a Sales Tool

Your listening ability is vital. Major companies—Sperry for example—are promoting the essentiality of listening with all of their thousands of employees, from the CEO to the newest clerk.

For a salesperson it is tough! We are exhorted to sell, sell, sell—tell 'em, show 'em, fast-talk 'em. We initiate action, and that requires talk. You have to constantly develop the judgmental acuity to know when to listen and how to listen more. Talk less—listen more.

Achieve Extra Power With Confidence

Your confidence requires constant refurbishing. It ebbs and flows. Nothing makes it flow better than abundant orders, the thrill of achievement, and growing remuneration. But life isn't like that all the time.

It's essential to build your confidence—bounce-back to pick you up off the floor after a string of losses. Some salespersons seek their confidence—bounce-back by exclaiming to their associates about how stupid those customers are. No way.

Customers Are Never Stupid

If that salesperson thinks a certain customer is stupid, that customer will know it. And will never buy.

And telling off the customer. Awful.

I once watched Larry C., a fairly promising salesperson, literally destroy himself by telling off the top buyer in a major New York advertising agency. After that ill-conceived attempt to rebuild his confidence by means of arrogant confrontation, he had to be let go. He had burned his bridges.

How to Guarantee Confidence

Here are six positive ways for you to achieve your confidence-bounce-back.

1. Assume that you are doing something wrong.
2. Reexamine and carefully study all facets of your sales methods.
3. Discuss your lost sales with a respected associate, your sales manager, and possibly your spouse.
4. Avoid justifying the losses by blaming the customers, blaming the competition, or putting the flaw to your product.
5. Find some sparkling-new elements to work into your selling.
6. And—it's simple, but infallible—augment your work schedule. Give it more hours, more thought, more calls. Reduce your pleasure time until you are firmly back on the track.

One approach not to use is sometimes suggested by a sales manager: "Go back to the buyers and ask them to please tell you frankly why they didn't buy from you." Never!

The salesperson's strong relationship with customers develops from the customer's respect for, belief in, and reliance upon the salesperson. Often there is a kind of mystique, too, working for the seller. To humbly seek sales guidance from the customer undermines all the long-term basics the salesperson is seeking to build with that customer.

As my former associate Joe C. used to put it, "I didn't get the order because I didn't sell it." He usually figured out how to sell the next order. His successful techniques earned him a handsome income.

Ten Commandments for Charisma

Remember the ten basics for cultivating your personal banner:

1. Face
2. Eyes
3. Eloquence
4. Voice
5. Enthusiasm
6. Gestures
7. Empathy

8. Attire
9. Listening
10. Confidence

Make it a habit to quickly rank yourself on each basic at least once a week. You will be gratified with the way this simple review will dramatically expand your selling achievement.

2. BUILD AN ELOQUENCE IN YOUR STYLE

We have spoken of eloquence before as one of ten elements of the basics list. It warrants a longer look.

Webster defines eloquence as "Discourse marked by force and persuasiveness." That's what we're after—force and persuasiveness towards achieving that winning edge in selling.

"Eloquence" may seem to imply fancy language and an oratorical presentation. Not so. In the winning kind of selling eloquence, it's a different use of language, a different slant of meaning, that adds a unique force and persuasiveness to your style.

Instead of "spend" use "invest." The two words have a totally different feel. "Spending" implies wasting; "investing" points to a wise dispensation of funds.

Mr. Marks, the jeweler, asked, "How much do you plan to invest in a diamond for your wife?" As far as I was concerned, it was spending. My wife wanted—yearned for—the diamond. It seemed frivolous. But she and Mr. Marks turned out to be right. Invest was the word. Definitely!

- Instead of "buy" use "acquire." An extra patina of value is added when you *acquire* a new car.
- *New*. A very forceful piece of eloquence. A new idea, a new product use, a new concept. Your adroit use of "new" says innovation and imagination.
- "Fantastic," "terrific," "gigantic," usually lead to careless overstatement, resulting in customer skepticism. Some salespersons erroneously consider those words eloquent. Understatement with words such as "fine," "suitable," "appropriate," "superior," etc., carry more real power and persuasion. That is eloquence.

There's Simplicity and Style in Eloquence

Slang and profanity have their place. You've undoubtedly known some cursers who made poetry out of profanity. You can't quite imagine a character like Will Rogers without slang. He was a winner, for sure. Recently I played golf with the chairman of one of America's top companies. The putts rimmed the cup, the balls landed behind trees, the bad bounces—all hard luck. His strongest epithets were "Nuts!" "Shucks!" "Awful!" He built his career through sales. You wouldn't have to ask him his judgment about profanity.

With most salespeople, profanity and slang do not add to their eloquence or their charisma or their winning edge. Unless you are that exceptional character who would stand naked without rough language, avoid it.

In the broadcasting business, ratings are the name of the game. Everyone talks about ratings. By contrast, one broadcaster I admired used the term "Audience Appreciation." His touch of eloquence made his ratings sound somewhat more valuable.

Make eloquence work for you with:

- Positive words, like "invest" instead of "spend"
- Persuasive understatement
- No slang or profanity

3. ADJUST YOUR SIX-WAY VOICE MECHANISM

It may seem contradictory to put so much emphasis on the use of your voice in adding extra charisma to your selling technique, when listening is often the greater need. But the application of your voice is more overt, whereas listening is more subtle, more intellectual, and, one must admit, often more valuable. Still, you have to state your case effectively . . . then listen.

I can't remember ever hearing a sales executive express the need to give thought to the different ways of using the voice. It was left to instinct, experience, chance. On uncountable occasions I stand in awe and envy of remarkable articulateness.

Far too many salespersons speak in a monotone. Dull. Yes, they're there, make a lot of calls, give good service, and are successful. But we're talking about techniques that tip the balance to *win more often.* I don't knock the monotone-voiced salesperson. I only claim that a better technique is to learn to use all the facets of your vocal instrument. It's there. Why waste it?

The Voice Sales Tool Is Adjustable

Your six-way voice transmission goes:

- Fast and slow
- Low and high
- Quiet and loud

That variety of voice gears offers quite a technique. Without question, no matter how well you use your voice in selling, you can improve it. Here's how:

1. Thinking about it—recognizing the value.
2. Desiring to improve this facet of your technique.
3. Using a tape recorder, listening and studying the verbalization of your selling.
4. Criticizing yourself.
5. Using the six-way voice more adroitly.

Typical fast-talking salespeople often come across as phony. Observe the rapid-fire TV or radio pitch. It is done loud and fast to sound more exciting and more enticing and to get more reason-why words into an expensive commercial.

You can't sell that way. But occasional fast bursts followed by slower and softer emphasis is effective. Likewise with low and high, quiet and loud.

John B. built one of the country's most successful sales organizations. I can still hear his words, "I think I'd rather hire a man who stutters occasionally than have a fast-talking, slick, insincere type."

Once I met an outstanding attorney who introduced himself with, "Hello, m-m-m-my n-name is Alan Jones. I st-st-stutter." It wasn't a gimmick, it was real. But he capitalized on it. In court, I was told, he would grope and stutter to get out a key word so that the judge and jury were all trying to say it for him . . . sympathetically.

How you talk won't replace knowledge, brains, and service. But it adds to the power, luster, and excitement of your selling.

How to Gain Understanding

Clear diction may not be a problem as far as you're concerned, but it is a serious problem for many salespersons. There are days for some of us when the words just don't come out right.

It is similar to an ineffective golf swing. The timing is off, swinging too fast, not waiting for the clubhead. Then we strain and try harder, but it gets worse. So, we seek a cue, a simple check, that helps make the swing work well more often.

The golf swing is a complex physical maneuver, but compared to the complexity of speech, it becomes simple. The basic tool of good speech involves a terribly intricate coordination of many small muscles of lips, tongue, cheeks, and throat.

I have a diction cue. It was a rhyme, taught me by a singing teacher. It works for me. Whenever I am preparing for a presentation or speech before a group of people, I go into a closet and repeat this rhyme several times.

> Limpid brooklets laughing gaily,
> Leap along like liquid light.
> Countless glittering dewbells falling,
> Lilt out lyrics of delight.
> Lads and lasses leave your loving,
> Leave the twilight's lazy glow.
> Leap along the leas with laughter,
> Lilting as the brooklets flow.

Silly? Perhaps. But it sure helped me sharpen my diction prior to hundreds of stand-up presentations. And it still helps.

Your winning edge in selling will expand with your income by giving a reasonable amount of attention to the way you use your voice.

Here are three easy exercises to remember:

1. Before you speak take a couple of deep breaths. Breathing is the motor of your voice, getting it started helps you speak better.

2. Hum to yourself a little before entering the customer's office. It improves your voice quality as it enhances your attitude.

3. Occasionally—in private—be like the old-time radio announcer: Cup your hand over your ear to hear yourself better. You will automatically make improvements.

4. GENERATING ESSENTIAL SELF-ESTEEM

You must *like* yourself. It's vital to building your winning edge in selling.

Self-esteem should not be confused with egotism, nor is it self-satisfaction. Self-esteem is liking yourself for what you are and what you do.

For example, if you procrastinate and put off a call that you know you should make, you like yourself a little less. Your self-esteem suffers. Any inadvertent acts of thoughtlessness, rudeness, or harsh words diminish one's self-esteem.

Recently in Miami I saw a young woman wearing a tee shirt with the legend "Nothing is Perfect." Personal perfection is not the objective. Generating your self-esteem is maintaining a happy balance of doing more things right than wrong.

Your self-esteem has a great deal to do with the level of your extra charisma. If you are unhappy with yourself, it is almost impossible to reflect even a small measure of charisma.

Remember, *you* are the product. Therefore, taking steps to ensure your having an adequate balance of positives to sustain a healthy self-esteem enhances your personal product.

Here's How You Do It

Seven positives to sustain your self-esteem:

1. Personal competence
2. Knowledge of product
3. Dependable performance
4. Strict integrity
5. Believing in your product and company

6. Controlling habits

7. Avoiding insensitive language

It's a rare human being who doesn't occasionally feel down and disillusioned. Too many positives are lacking. A brief review of the seven positives will stand you in good stead when you feel that your self-esteem is at a low level.

5. STRENGTHEN YOUR SALES VOCABULARY WITH THESE SEVEN IDEAS

Build your winning edge with these concepts:

1. Winning things to say

2. Saying them the best way

3. Eradicating five losers

4. Being a stickler for accuracy

5. Using slogans that sell

6. Implementing the power of W-H-Y

7. Knowing the seven verbal sins

More sales from a better vocabulary? Absolutely! Your study and implementation of these successful techniques will positively tip the balance for you.

It is axiomatic that what you say and how you say it—as well as what you do *not* say—wins or loses every time. Unless your product is a vital monopoly, or you just happen to be there at a time when the customer urgently needs what you have to sell. That's all right, too. *Being there* is in itself winning selling. I never had anything against easy orders. Love 'em!

Winning Things to Say

- State the benefit.
- Offer an idea.
- Use key words and phrases such as: "Here's a positive investment to make you money." "Just look at these plusses." "It's good." "It fits." "It's quality." "It's a value."

Short, terse affirmatives. Use them.

One of the better sales reps in my company, Bill M., had a technique that worked very well for him. After stating several short affirmatives, he'd smile and say softly "and that's the truth."

Say It With Optimism

Optimism is a marvelous force. Remember the saying: "Optimists have more fun, but pessimists are right more often"? Don't believe it! Making optimism work for you is a highly successful technique. Optimism is contagious. You must exhibit a full-flowing optimism that you are going to get that order. Optimism is a big part of closing. Without optimists there would be no jet planes, no television, no air conditioning, no inside plumbing—no major progress.

Furthermore, optimism is more fun!

Five Losers to Eradicate

1. Clichés. They are weak because they are worn thin from overuse.

2. Weak words. Tentatives such as "maybe," "I guess."

3. Overstatement: "Fantastic," "terrific," "sensational."

4. Trivia. The weather, the hobbies, the family.

5. Excessive or inappropriate slang or profanity.

Use Slogans That Sell

THINK—the IBM slogan.

W. Clement Stone, the dynamic insurance executive, applies slogans lavishly and with great success. Strangely, there exists a reticence on the part of many sales organizations and salespersons to use slogans. They erroneously fear seeming corny. Mostly they lack imagination. Their lack is your opportunity. For a salesperson to proclaim to a customer "Honesty Is Our Policy" is a cliché; and it is indeed corny and begs skepticism. However, that doesn't rule out certain strong and pertinent slogans.

Raymond S., the advertising genius who created "Serutan,

natures spelled backwards," had a slogan framed on the wall behind his desk. It read: "There are no such things as foolish questions. Only foolish answers." It invited inquiry and invited ideas.

Building your inventory of potent slogans stems from your imagination. A whole fabric of slogans, original and borrowed, was woven into my sales company:

- We'll never be so much smarter that we don't have to work harder than any competitor.
- Always underpromise and overfulfill.
- The inventory of ideas is limitless.
- Much of the world's work is done by ill people.
- Praise in public, criticize in private.
- "Imagination is more important than knowledge"— Albert Einstein.

Effective sloganizing adds power and punch to your sales vocabulary.

Implement the Power of W-H-Y

Using one simple word, *why*, adroitly and sparingly, is a strong winning technique. A soft-voiced "Why, Fred, why that objection?" may induce Fred to explain, and to tear down his own objections in the process. *Why* brings the objections into the open, to be answered and overcome.

An occasional full sales meeting could be well spent on the adroit and creative application of that one simple, powerful little word, *why*.

The Seven Verbal Sins

- "To be perfectly frank"
- "And to tell the truth"
- "Now, confidentially"
- "Sincerely" and "Honestly"
- "That is not so"
- "I disagree"

- "You're wrong"

Eliminating these, or any semblance thereof, from your sales vocabulary is vital.

6. CREATE THE LUSTER OF LUCK

Making luck happen for you more often is easy. It's easy because good luck is not an accident. Being lucky is largely a matter of giving luck every opportunity to happen to you.

The other day at golf, an opponent was radiating the luster of luck. His shots hit trees and bounced close to the pin. Chip shots and long putts rolled into the cup. It kept on happening for 18 holes. Why was he so very lucky? Easy. When it began to happen, he expected it to continue. He stayed loose and relaxed. Luck is a product of perseverance rather than providence. A good old slogan: "The harder you work, the luckier you get."

Creating the luster of luck for your winning edge in selling will positively happen if you let it. I can hear the president of my former company laughing and saying, "Hey, don't tell me about your bad luck, I'm lucky!" Competitors look at him, with his luster of luck and his substantial income and enviously agree, "He sure is lucky!" He made it that way. Long ago he learned that wearing the luster of luck makes it happen more often.

Summary

Win big with extra charisma by building these strong elements into your selling:

I. Carefully cultivate *your personal banner*. *You* are the product.
II. Build an *eloquence* in your style. The force and persuasion that tips the balance.
III. Adjusting your *six-way voice* mechanism. Fast and slow; high and low; quiet and loud.
IV. *Package* your personal product. Enhance your personal style.
V. Generate *essential self-esteem*. Apply those seven positives to maintain your balance of self-esteem.

VI. Use seven ideas to *strengthen your sales vocabulary*. What to say and what not to say to win more often.

VII. Expand your charisma with your *luster of luck*. Just let luck happen.

If seven is lucky—and it definitely is!—using the seven basics of this chapter will sharpen your winning edge and increase your income substantially.

2 HOW YOU CAN STIMULATE YOUR CLIENTS WITH CREATIVE SELLING

- Nurture creativity from imagination power
- Discover exciting new ideas that make sales happen
- Build richness and added pleasure from the extra drama of creative selling

YOUR SIX STEPS TO EXPAND CREATIVE SELLING

1. Lead with an idea
2. Find new ways to make ideas happen
3. Excite customer interest and participation with ideas
4. Use these six winning ways to augment your idea inventory
5. Work creative listening into creative selling
6. Use creative selling, not price-cutting

Out there on the firing line you're in charge. The action comes from you. You hold the controls towards one objective: the sale. The purest money-making process in selling stems from your ability to generate ideas that sell.

1. LEAD WITH AN IDEA

Every product, every service, and every scientific or artistic development originated from an idea. Your ideas use your product or service to solve problems for your customer.

- Ideas are exciting!
- Ideas command attention!
- Ideas stimulate ideas!
- Ideas stimulate action!
- Ideas create business!

Ideas, especially your *lead ideas*, are indeed the fuel of creative selling.

Creative Selling Comes in Different Sizes

1. Any idea or concept or angle that induces a larger use of your product is creative.
2. You'll be applauded for an unusual use of your product that would not have happened except for your creative sales intervention.
3. Super creative selling is that which creates a whole new category of business—such as a bicycle retailer starting a bike club, using his bikes.

Creative is creative, large or small. Your idea is the seed.

Some people fear ideas. They don't wish to see the status quo disturbed. You need to couch your approach to this individual so that it won't rock the boat. Make it a "suggestion" or a "thought" or a "different slant." It's both the nature of your lead and *how* you lead with your idea that enables creative selling to sharpen your winning edge and build more revenue for you.

Remember, there's hardly ever a bad idea; the only truly bad idea is the absence of any idea. Nothing happens in a vacuum.

Judgment tempers your idea lead. If you are unsure of the customer's reaction to your opening idea, come on easy with something like, "Mr. Evans, this may be a crazy idea, but I've got to tell you about it." That opening often evokes a reaction such as, "That's not so crazy," or, "It sure is crazy, but . . ." That "but" frequently will lead to an adaptation of your idea. And that "but" has action going.

Adjust your idea lead to fit the actual scope of the idea. Is it a genuine *big* idea? Or more an adaptation, a "suggestion," or a "thought"? Also adjust the idea opener to your customer's attitude, sense of humor, and usual receptivity to innovation. Does the customer enjoy new ideas, or is he or she a skeptic?

Some Do It This Way

One super salesman in the radio advertising business created $12,000 worth of commissions for himself out of one idea sale. He said: ". . . everything starts within the attitudinal position . . . power begins to reverberate . . . they sense the power you possess. The sale was creative. One of my best." It all started from an idea lead.

Hugh T., one of the country's hottest insurance salespeople—for four years top producer of one of the giant companies—sells *grandchildren policies*. Is that a hot idea? You bet it is, if you're where there's an abundance of grandparents. You tailor your idea to fit the market.

Bill B., a great salesman—he's now president of his company—used the flamboyant idea entry. He'd dash into the customer's office with his product insignia pasted on his forehead, throw his coat on the floor, and shout "Henry, I've one hell of an idea for you!"

Wayne J., another insurance salesperson, attributes his

remarkable success to, "I just sit close, talk soft, and don't take no for an answer."

Then there's the straight idea lead: "Good morning, Gladys. Good to see you. Here's an idea just for you." Show your excitement over the idea about to be unveiled. It's contagious. Your idea leads hold the promise of solving a problem.

The alternative to an idea lead is "whitlin' talk" or nongermane trivia. Think how often in the course of the day the customer hears, "How's your golf? How's your family? How's business?" The fact is, many of your competitors come on dull. Let it be their exclusive specialty, while you come on with excitement—leading with an idea.

2. FIND NEW WAYS TO MAKE IDEAS HAPPEN

You think about that customer's needs and probable problems. Let it bother you, worry you, if the idea won't come. It will. Maybe at 3 a.m. it strikes. Great! I-M-A-G-I-N-A-T-I-O-N. You've got it, or you wouldn't be reading this book. Your imagination is your most powerful sales weapon.

You stretch your imagination to stretch your remuneration. Imagination was never intended to substitute for facts, research, or other pertinent information. The application of imagination allows you to juggle and sift all of your data until it falls into place in a way that shoots you out of the office with an I-D-E-A to close another big sale.

Recently a very choice piece of business languished in the wallows. The decision dangled for days. It could go one way or another any moment. Instead of sitting and stewing or pacing and praying, the sales manager said, "Let's do something." Something! Anything! They sent a singing telegram. They sent flowers with a choice cryptic sales phrase. They sent gimmicks, such as a roulette wheel with "Why Gamble"? Corny? Sure. But it was action instead of inaction. While the competitors stewed and paced, these superstars turned on their imaginations. And they landed a gorgeous contract.

Imagination Builds Brain Power

Imagination is like a muscle, growing stronger with use. Did you ever hear of a strained, sprained, or sore imagination? It's an infinite source, like a bottomless well: The more you drain it, the sweeter the water.

Five ways to put more ideas into your creative selling:

1. Think. Think hard about the customer's needs and problems. Find ideas that will help.

2. Build ideas with imagination by using it constantly.

3. Visualize your imagination as a vast reservoir of creative selling ideas.

4. Know that your imagination coupled with energy is truly fantastic power.

5. Gain winning advantage from the realization that, despite imagination's abundance, few salespeople work it.

3. EXCITE CUSTOMER INTEREST AND PARTICIPATION WITH IDEAS

Your creative selling begins with an idea, born out of your imagination and launched in a manner to earn the interest of your customer or prospect. It's launched with your voice—that six-way voice machine: fast, slow, high, low, soft, loud. You want to be certain that you give your idea the best possible setting. Should you shout it, whisper it, state it slowly and emphatically? A moment of extra mental rehearsal on the way to the customer's office will add to the luster of your idea and ensure that it attracts more interest.

You have probably been frustrated on many occasions when you seemed unable to get the prospect to appreciate a certain somewhat obscure value in your product. Often the close depends on a hidden value.

In my company we used "diamonds" to demonstrate perception or discernment of exceptional qualitative values. We placed about six rhinestones in front of the customer on a black velvet pad. Then the salesperson proffered a gold pen, inviting the customer to "pick out the diamond." As the customer nudged the stones about, the salesperson pointed out: "The rhinestones are worth about fifty cents; the diamond, four thousand dollars. Quite a difference! And it's all a matter

of discernment . . . recognizing a subtle value." Then the salesperson let the customer off the hook with, "Of course, you
recognize those are all rhinestones, *but* . . ." and related it to
the recognition of the significant and obscure value of our
product.

Excite your customers' interest by:

1. Having some rehearsal behind your planned verbalization.
2. Getting to your idea quickly.
3. Applying an illustrative prop, if readily available and
   appropriate.

Customer participation in your idea is vital. If the customer's
eyes show interest, you encourage participation with something like "Neat, isn't it?" If he or she kind of shrugs, offer
"What do you think?" If the reaction is a yawn, try "How
would you change it?" Whatever the reaction, nudge the customer with a question to get him or her to participate in your
idea.

"It stinks!" is a response you risk, but at least you have a
reaction that is potentially productive. At worst, your effort
banks a bit of gratitude factor toward your ultimate benefit.
The customer knows you've thought about the problem and
tried. It's not a total failure.

You shouldn't be too concerned about the rejections. All
innovators face that. Any time you are discouraged about an
idea that fizzled, think about your competitors whose contribution was:

- "Hi, Gladys. Got anything for me?" Or
- "Hey, Gladys, when you gonna buy me?" Or
- "Heck, Gladys, I gotta have an order!"

It's all "me" and "I," whereas your method is all "you." You
know which approach is going to pay off for you.

Good selling is *giving*, never taking. Your winning edge
in selling involves an abundance of giving. A kind of golden
rule? Okay.

- You *give* ideas

- You *give* enthusiasm
- You *give* encouragement
- You *give* optimism
- You *give* personal attention
- You *give* thorough follow-through
- You *give* super service
- You don't even "take" orders, you *place* orders, you *receive* orders.

The ultimate in idea participation is when *your* idea becomes *our* idea.

A large southern company located in an out-of-the-way town indicated the possibility of a rather substantial piece of business. It notified several suppliers. All but one mailed in stacks of data and promotion. But Ed W. used a different approach: He presented his idea enthusiastically, graphically, and *in person*. At the conclusion of his creative presentation, the prospect pointed to the stacks of mailed-in material on a table and said "Ed, I don't have to go through all that stuff. I like *our* idea." My friend *earned* all of the business.

In creative selling, as in sports, much of your opportunity accrues from the mistakes of your competition.

But even if it's a nice clear day and all of your competitors are there with good products and fire in their eyes, you have a winning edge if you can get the prospect involved in *your* idea.

That's creative selling!

Your competitors will tell you, and each other, how lucky you were!

My father told me, "Ideas are a dime a dozen, it's execution that counts." How true. Recently, in digging through his marvelous sales letters, I found this: ". . . ideas like diamonds are dug out in the rough, and it takes some discrimination to tell a diamond from a common stone."

As you proliferate ideas and use them in your creative selling, and as you build the knack of establishing customer participation in "our" idea, your skill at execution (including killing the competition) expands limitlessly.

A marvelously creative salesperson, Charlie C., in an aggressive advertising company, had been admonished, "Sell at the top!" and "Never take no from a man who doesn't have the authority to say yes." Good advice. He believed it. But he was spinning his wheels with the top brass at one company. They didn't grasp his idea. Then he heard about a youngster—a beginner almost—who was highly regarded by the top execs in the company as a comer. Charlie C. tried a new tack with an old idea: A Trojan horse.

The young man listened closely to Charlie. When he thoroughly grasped the idea, he eagerly embraced it as *our* idea. This inside emissary became the creative salesman's salesman and delivered a fine order plus five successive renewals!

For more big sales on your commission statement get *customer participation* in your creative selling. Here's how:

1. Rehearse it.
2. Launch it.
3. Prop it.
4. Sell by giving, not taking.
5. Cultivate "our" idea.
6. Be alert for "Trojan horses."

4. SIX WINNING WAYS TO AUGMENT YOUR IDEA INVENTORY

1. Know that culling ideas from your imagination pays off big
2. Steal ideas
3. Keep an idea pad on your desk and in your pocket
4. Direct your thinking away from the ordinary toward the extraordinary
5. Find your exclusive degrees of definable differences
6. Use special risk insurance to add quality to your idea inventory

There's Always a Hot Idea

You probably share my astonishment over how many people wearing the label of salesperson fear the unexplored territory of innovative idea selling. It's a well-kept secret that those unfrequented areas are fun, exciting, and rewarding—for your wallet and your personal achievement. Possibly it's gilding the obvious to point out the need to affirm the personal pleasure rewards, in addition to the cash. But with the preponderance of salespeople in all fields who seem to actually avoid ideas, stressing the enjoyment to be found in being a creative idea person is essential.

Do it—enjoy it!

A Bit of Thievery Adds Savor

Originality may often be overrated. It's strange how people resist stealing someone else's good idea. It's not patented, but it *is* tested.

At one time my company had a great winning presentation going. It was bringing in millions of dollars of new business. In a burst of generosity at a meeting, I offered the full presentation, at negligible out-of-pocket cost, to *all* our competitors. I told them, "We'll take our label off, you put yours on." Our intent was to broaden the exposure of this fine presentation, to increase its proven value, and to create more business for all.

Yet not one single competitor gave one single exposure of that superb presentation to anyone. Nor did any one of them build a presentation of their own.

We said, "Here it is, steal it."

No! It wasn't their idea. An appropriate epithet comes to mind when you ponder the fact that about forty so-called sales companies preferred to languish in a vacuum than to borrow a tested idea . . . freely given.

If your inventory of original ideas is running low, look about and steal. Adapt, improve on any number of ideas lying out there for the taking. You won't be sued—they aren't patented!

A Paper Reminder

It's too simple. You probably do it. If not, give it a try: Keep an idea pad on your desk and in your pocket. The effort is minimal and the rewards are substantial.

To add some fun and utility put a bit of pizzaz into it with a symbol printed at the top of the pad. A light bulb, a tea kettle, a smoking cranium, a safety pin, a cloud—anything to signify ideas and imagination. The symbol is self-inducement. Also, you will undoubtedly use the pad as a visual for part of your idea selling, in addition to having it to jot down an idea whenever it strikes you.

Dare to Be Different

Putting more productive power into your creative selling requires some risk. You can't be concerned or timid because it's never been done before or the idea seems crazy or too unusual on your first appraisal of it. Only when your idea-building is allowed to meander through totally new channels do you open up your maximum chances to discover a new winning idea.

My craziest idea came out of desperation. Business conditions were deplorable. A few small orders—crumbs—were all we could scrounge out of the marketplace. We put together a huge bulk buy at a high price. The reaction: "Crazy, ridiculous, it can't work." But it *did* work, and remarkably well, because:

1. No competitor had anything comparable, and they snorted disdainfully at the thought of imitating our crazy idea.

2. It flew in the face of the times, asking for $100,000 when the norm was scrambling for $1,000.

3. We gained more of the available small orders in the process of fostering the bold approach.

4. It gave the salespeople stature and bridged them over a difficult time.

5. This creative selling concept put extra dollars in our

pockets. We actually sold some of the big, "unsale-able," crazy deals and we greedily garnered all of the little orders in the process.

We had the guts and creativity to sell big and proud, when everybody else was singing the blues with a tin cup in hand. But it all started from a very crazy, irresponsible, and unwork-able idea. We turned our thinking away from the ordinary toward the extraordinary with a monstrous concept. It was the beginning of the opening of our imaginations. One creative effort led to another, and another. These waves of creative selling built a momentum which propelled that company to an unchallenged pinnacle position in the industry.

Brainstorming is a tested way to work a group imagina-tion. The group is uninhibited in blurting out whatever comes to mind about a specific sales problem. They scribble and shout, and eventually a gem of an idea is heard.

It's the Differences that Sell

Joe C., one of the most brilliant salespersons in my experience, originated, cultivated, and assiduously applied "The Definable Degree of Difference." Differences were what he sold, and they all originated from ideas. It was what made Joe "lucky" in the eyes of the less creative. Inevitably his income multiplied—by twenty times in one decade. He became the highest-earning salesperson in his field.

What's different is usually better. Definable degrees of difference are mined out of your imagination to give your prod-uct different applications:

1. To give your client different ideas that help him or her.

2. To make him or her want to help you.

3. To give your product a certain extra winning aura of value.

These differences do work, miraculously. A salesperson of that dull gray metal, lead, contended, "Lead is lead. My lead is no different from anyone else's. They buy personalities, friends, and because of gifts and entertainment." Another lead salesperson, Charles E., earned an edge for his lead by applying some simple creative ideas:

- He created an informative and humorous mailing under the printed heading ". . . Get the lead out."
- He made up some lead paper weights with customers' signatures on them.
- He created some grotesque lead nickels.

These were only part of a stream of ideas which made his lead more desirable than that of his cynical competitor.

Work up Some Risk Insurance

Find someone to bounce your ideas off of. It may be a spouse, a sales manager, a friend—but be certain you have the right person to evaluate your creativity constructively.

A spouse might fear you're putting your neck out. Some miscast sales managers are wet blankets. They want the selling done their way with no fancy changes. But a wise sales manager is the best of all sounding boards. A trade deal with an equally creative salesperson is good: You examine each other's ideas.

Pitfalls to avoid:

- The super enthusiast who applauds any idea
- The pessimist who dislikes the disruption of the status quo
- The critic who feels obliged to demolish your idea

You will find your best idea risk insurance in a contemplative individual possessed of that marvelous quality called judgment. Chances are such a person won't give you a quick reaction or an unstudied negative response. He or she may later pose a few questions which cause you to refine your idea.

My super sounding board never condemned nor grimaced nor enthused. Initially, he listened quietly. If I went back a second time, he asked a question or two. When I persisted for a third time, he joined his ideas with mine and we usually had a selling winning edge. Often I didn't go back a second time because I realized, and he realized, that the idea was flawed. It died a quiet death.

Your idea stands a better chance of creating more sales if it has simmered awhile in a fine mind. Many of your ideas will be so obvious that they do not require an aging process. You run with them. But the big, unusual, and exciting concept frequently improves through application of risk insurance.

5. WORK CREATIVE LISTENING INTO CREATIVE SELLING

Creative selling and creative listening are parallel and reciprocal activities. You can't have one without the other. Your achievement of creative listening is tremendously vital to expanding creative selling to unlimited heights of income.

Very rarely will you observe a truly creative listener. This rarity is to be expected. Your entire background, your company attitude, your sales meetings, all promote product advantages, statements, demonstrations, words, and ideas. These are to be proclaimed, exhorted, and shouted from the housetops. Fast-talkers are often accepted as good salespeople. Sometimes they are.

No One Can Say Yes When You're Talking

Creative listening may be the most difficult attribute in the development of creative selling. Most of us, when we listen, are thinking about what we are going to say next. How frequently do you meet a new person and moments later realize you have forgotten that individual's name?

I'll confess creative listening is and always has been my principal shortcoming. In a Chinese fortune cookie I found: "When I listen I learn, when I talk I only tell what I know." I carried it in my wallet for years. It probably helped.

You've heard all kinds of preachment and platitudes about listening. Let me give you four simple aids:

1. Put up a LISTEN sign in your office and inside your briefcase.

2. Take notes. It forces you to listen more closely.

3. Have some pads printed with a big ear and "LISTEN" at the top. Use them for note-taking and later to summarize what you heard.

4. Don't miss a single name. Concentrate. As soon as possible write the other person's name. Then remember it.

This exercise is as good as any I know to increase your listening aptitude.

Use the Ears at Least as Much as the Voice

My company made a sizable investment in creative-listening selling. We built an attractive private dining room with a crystal chandelier and an oriental rug. A haute-cuisine chef and a meticulous server provided a delectable repast. The view was New York's spectacular Rockefeller Plaza.

The salesperson posed a simple question to the guest executive: "In general, Mr. Mortimer, what is your company's outlook on media at the present time?" Then our people listened and listened and listened. Afterwards they made notes on what they had learned.

Hardly without exception, the guest was willing—almost eager—to express in detail the best way to make a sale of our product, spot radio advertising, to his company. This listening project paid off in untold millions of dollars of new business. The unmeasured by-product was that each of our salespeople became better creative listeners and, accordingly, better creative salespersons. Of course, this dining room facility had many other creative applications. We called it a "sales stage."

6. USE CREATIVE SELLING, NOT PRICE-CUTTING

As you know, some price selling is creative. Clever rate structures, discounts, and combinations require creativity. They make the value more alluring. Anyone who is stiff-necked about using price as a sales tool has his or her head in the sand.

But flat-out price-cutting to get the order is uncreative. The salesperson who dangles a price cut is expected to cut the next time, and the next time. It's a trap.

Your mode of creative selling helps to make your product

more valuable. This won't remove you from price wars by any
means, but it will improve your survival rate. In addition to
price, you have these nine winning key words going for you:

1. Ideas
2. Excitement
3. Participation
4. Contribution
5. Imagination
6. Thinking
7. Giving
8. Unusual
9. Listening

When you lead with an intriguing idea and generate excitement
and customer involvement, the ultimate element of price of
cost is less important. Your competitor, who only plays price,
will get some orders. However, flagrant price-cutting makes
his or her business less and less profitable to the company.
Somewhere in the chain of transactions, the company either
develops creative selling or goes out of business.

At one time price and price-cutting became the only game
in the automobile business. The exception was "our service,"
frequently touted as justifying extra price. If you bought that,
you usually found their service was no better than you'd
known at "Cut-Rate Joe." Furthermore you paid full price for
the service.

A dealer friend of mine, Fred R., decided to step outside
the price arena by creatively selling *appeal* at a time when
most car dealer's shirt-sleeve salespeople stood around in the
showroom waiting for customers to walk in for "The best deal
in town."

My friend insisted that his salespeople dress especially
attractively. He put all but one of them in gorgeous new cars,
all a rich shade of red with a black top, white sidewalls, wire
wheels, and black upholstery. The advertising featured beauty,
style, comfort—no mention of price.

The salespeople drove slowly through selected neighborhoods every day for two weeks. The beautiful cars were noticed. Each day the salespeople stopped to see friends or acquaintances. "We thought you might like to see our new car," they'd say, pointing to it in the driveway, "Isn't it beautiful?"

The word of mouth spread. The creative demonstration and pride in product, versus the rest of the market shouting "We're cheaper!" was highly successful. Fred sold more cars than anyone else in town and at a higher profit per unit. And he provided superior service because he could afford to.

Summary

Tip the balance in your favor with creative selling:

   I. Open your presentation with an idea
  II. Develop ways to make ideas happen
 III. Excite customer interest and participation
 IV. Expand your inventory of ideas
  V. Apply creative listening
 VI. Use creative selling versus price-cutting.

Your constant awareness and cultivation of these six aspects of creative selling will positively make you a more effective salesperson. You will close more sales more quickly. There is no limit to your creative potential. There is no limit to your earning potential.

3 HOW YOU BUILD A WINNING EDGE THROUGH PERSUASIVE PRESENTATIONS

- Gain extra sales by means of strong presentations
- Learn the best techniques to make presentations most effective
- Realize the values of prestige and personal-stature growth with effective presentations

YOUR KEYS TO POTENT PRESENTATIONS

1. Apply effective, exciting visual techniques

2. Discover those verbal ideas that tip the balance

3. Use five winning methods for reading, improvising, paraphrasing

4. Learn new concepts for using drama and staging

5. Build strong systems for adapting and rehearsing presentations to best fit your prospect.

The super sales power of unique, dramatic, convincing presentations will increase your income, elevate your stature, and vastly augment the satisfaction to be derived from your selling career.

Why presentations? That's like asking: Why salespersons? Presentations are a vital sales tool. They complement and assist salespersons, and build good salespersons into exceedingly better ones.

There are a wide variety of presentation techniques. All are potentially valuable. Some will fit you better than others. We'll be talking about that. It's essential that you become comfortable with the methods you use.

The most important thing about presentations is that you have them and use them effectively.

Imagination is the springboard to all presentations, regardless of the techniques applied. As you know very well, imagination everywhere is in short supply. Take selling real estate, for example. A house—a home—is an enticing, imaginative, emotional product. Every prospect projects herself or himself into or out of a certain house.

The J.B. Realty Sales Company *shows houses*. The Frederick C. Realty Company *sells homes*. The difference? Imagination—presentation. Over and beyond the basics of fitting the homes to be seen to the customer's family, finances, school, and tastes, the Frederick C. Realty Company makes a modest investment (the potential commission adequately justifies it) in a unique presentation system.

Back in the real estate office, after the home-inspection tour, Frances, the promotion manager of the Frederick C. Realty Company, leads the prospects into a comfortable conference room where she personally delivers about a ten-minute slide presentation.

Colorful slides, carefully selected and sequenced, build a strong endorsement element by showing people of similar tastes and means to those of the prospects living happily in

59

homes purchased through The Frederick C. Realty Company.

It might come across as high-pressure selling if it weren't for its professional thoroughness. It is basic selling, with no stone left unturned, by application of a fine presentation system. The Frederick C. Realty Company *sells* homes. Most of its competitors just show houses.

Seven reasons for creating and using sales-winning presentations:

1. You increase your sales and income substantially.
2. You gain efficiency through preorganizing your facts.
3. You add drama to your style.
4. You retain product knowledge more readily.
5. You become more articulate.
6. You grow in stature.
7. You vastly expand your winning edge over all competitors.

There's that lucky seven again—seven sound reasons for you to use presentations as a means to make you luckier!

1. APPLY EXCITING VISUAL TECHNIQUES

All human appeal and communication is through the senses: sight, sound, taste, smell, touch. Much selling relies excessively on sound . . . the sound of the salesperson's voice, often overly oral and too little aural! A sixth sense definitely fits into the winning edge concept of selling. This sixth sense can be many things. It's judgment. It's empathy. It's common sense, or should we call it uncommon sense. It's imagination. It's luck, too.

Sight Leads the Parade

Visual techniques receive top billing in presentations; just as "sight" is usually first in any listing of the five senses. To fully appreciate the potency of sight, you need only consider the impact of television on people's lives and habits. Our objective is to examine the various visual techniques that may be available to you.

In dealing with sensual stimulators, it is easy to get carried away. The excitement is contagious. Your perception will stay balanced if you adhere to the following five goals in your utilization and selection of the most appropriate visual techniques:

1. Seek to convince your prospect.
2. Organize a convincing chain of logical elements.
3. Dramatize those elements to heighten interest.
4. Build a funnel of facts to create desire.
5. Convert the desire to the sale.

The above underlying conceptual sequence is important to keep in mind. Otherwise the show itself can overbalance the selling direction. That is a hazard in presentation techniques. They can become so fanciful and complex that the salesperson begins to visualize himself or herself primarily as an entertainer.

Choosing Your Visual Techniques

The choice of what's best for you is a wide one. Part of the selection depends upon what fits you best—that which you use most comfortably. The presentation leads most readily to that bottom line—the sale—if you are at ease in giving it.

Let's examine seven visual devices:

1. Films
2. Slides
3. Photos
4. Booklets
5. Letters
6. Signs
7. Flesh and blood

All of these may be—and probably should be—used at some time or other in varying selling circumstances.

Film is a powerful medium. Many companies use it to dramatize product use, manufacturing methods, and the overall scope of the company. If your company has a great film and it fits your customers and prospects, of course you'll use it and capitalize on it to the fullest extent.

In most person-to-person, or even group presentations, I have an aversion to film because all you do is flip the switch. Of course, the nature of your preamble and follow-up can make a film presentation more effective and more personalized.

However, those techniques which put more of you into the sales equation are usually the best ones. Otherwise, how can presentations contribute to *your* winning edge?

Slides. You'll recognize my prejudice. It's hard to beat the flexibility, adaptability, and personalization of slide presentations. A well-planned slide presentation affords strong sales impact because the salesperson's words accompany the flow of the slides. In this regard, a taped spiel synchronized with the slides is a poor stand-in for you.

Tape Is a Detraction

My good friend, Norm G., produces some very fine trade publications. His sales manager was showing me their slide presentation. "It's heavy," was his first comment. It *was* heavy, with the combination of projector and tape-player. Obviously such a cumbersome presentation is a deterrent against its frequent use by the sales staff.

The sales manager hooked up all the parts and flipped the switch. The totally mechanical presentation ran by itself. His second comment was, "Well, there it is. What do you think?"

It was disappointing. *A potent sales presentation must deeply involve the salesperson.* A major value in a presentation is the way it serves to augment *your* effectiveness. It is never meant to replace the salesperson. The necessary rehearsal required to develop facility with the presentation adds greatly to your talents.

You Mold the Pitch to the Prospect

Slides provide flexibility, whereas a film is static. You select those slides that best fit the interests of your customer. You then sequence them to the desired flow of facts and ideas. Then you organize your words to tie it together.

For several years I worked in New York and all over the country with a simple, mechanical, virtually fool-proof slide projector. All I needed was an audience of one or more persons and a white wall. It was simple and effective.

Later we sought more complex—supposedly more dramatic—techniques. They were cumbersome and failed.

Recently, in New York, one of my former associates invited me to view their new presentation. It was superb! Charlie C. gave it in his own sincere, knowledgeable words to accompany very attractive and convincing illustrations emanating from a simple, reliable slide projector.

The significance of simplicity!

Slides use *you*. You are the sound accompanying the sight. Your winning edge grows in the process.

Pictures Are Potent

Studying ads in magazines and newspapers will increase your perception of which photos and illustrations make the strongest impression.

A certain sequence of *photos*, accompanying your verbal presentation, lends conviction and interest to an informal, across-the-desk presentation. *Booklets* combining text and illustrations can be a worthwhile sales tools. However, they are best as a leave-behind—a confirmation.

Two insurance salespeople of my acquaintance, although separated by years and miles, each used a booklet and read every word over my shoulder. Dull selling! Booklet presentations are often cold and impersonal. The persuasion, force, and charisma that emanate from *you* is lacking.

Say It With Music

Good words sing, and exceptional *sales letters* can provide a provocative melody. It depends on how well you write. Sales letters usually serve best for confirmation or follow-up. Bill T., highly successful advertising and securities salesperson, used hand-written one-liners very effectively. He knew the value of letters and also the negative effect of long, wordy ones.

A Strong Eye-Catcher

Remember how a certain roadside sign grabbed your attention? 'Signs have a powerful role in selling. Think of all variety of signs—good and bad—that announce retail establishments.

A business card is a sign. Likewise the notepaper head-lined "From the Mind of Bill Jones" (not the cliché: "From the Desk of . . .") or "From the Imagination of . . ." or "Here's an Idea . . ." Make yours original.

Walking into the customer's office with a sign occasion-ally is an attention-grabber. It gets to the point quickly with your key fact and will usually elicit an appreciative chuckle from your prospect.

| 32% Gain! |
| 21% Gain! |
| 44% Gain! |
| YOURS ? |

Live Flesh-and-Blood Come-Ons

One of the best. We were after a big, new, highly prestigious client. A huge giant toting a sandwich sign on the Avenue of the Americas in New York City was hired as the prop for our presentation. We dressed him in cape and top hat. As the eye-popping opener, our monster strode alone into the room with the waiting client group. They were agape. Our genial giant seemed ten feet tall. After an appropriate interval, he swirled open his cape to reveal the message "FOR GIANT SALES GAINS, GO EASTMAN." We made the sale.

My best "flesh-and-blood" presentation was at a Regional National Association of Broadcasters meeting at the University of Alabama. In advance, I requested the assistance of the three loveliest female students, a blonde, a brunette and a redhead.

My presentation espoused the radio medium. I wanted to prove that radio, like magazines and television, is a full-color medium. To illustrate my point, I described flames coming out the windows of a burning building and the vivid fall foliage in Vermont. But the real clincher was the three young women, concealed backstage. They were absolutely gorgeous! The audience was mostly men. I insisted that they all close their eyes and imagine the most scrumptious blonde possible. "Let your imagination run wild."

Then, with their eyes still closed, I said, "Now I'm going to prove how your imagination is more potent than reality and how effectively you have imagined the gold of her hair, the radiance of her complexion, the loveliness of her figure." I paused. "Miss Jones will you please step forward."

They opened their eyes and gasped. She was truly a rare beauty. I said, "Now, you see, as lovely as Miss Jones is, she cannot compare to the woman you imagined."

"Are you out of your mind!" The shout from the audience came as one, accompanied with gales of laughter.

Twice more, with the brunette and the redhead, I played the same game, with the same response. The point was made: You do imagine in color. (On this occasion, though, the real thing topped the imagination!)

The next speaker, pitching television, spread his hands and said, "How do I top that?"

It's Fun—But Get to Your Objective

Applying unusual visual techniques puts you on stage in a strong dramatic spotlight. Your competence in these roles gives you a positive winning edge over competitors, but keep firmly in mind that it's all a *funnel* leading to one thing: *The Sale.*

2. DISCOVER THOSE VERBAL IDEAS THAT TIP THE BALANCE

You. Y-O-U. There is no stronger verbal idea. It bears repetition:

"What have you got for *me*?"

"Why didn't you buy *me*?"

"Anything for *me* today, Joe?"

"*I'd* sure like to sell you . . ."

"I've just got to get your business . . ."

All negative. You do the positive: Open with "you."

"You won't believe it."

"You're about to view . . ."

"Wait till *you* see."

"You'll be astonished . . ."

"Bill, you've been waiting. . . ."

All too frequently in sales letters every paragraph opens with "I." "I think," "I appreciate," "I advise," "I hope," "I'll await," etc. Strange as it may seem, every use of "I" is readily converted to "you." It's just a matter of thinking "you" instead of "I." Like: "You will be interested," "Will you please," "You expressed," etc.

The "I" syndrome vanished from our company after a few carbon copies of letters were returned to the writer with his "I's" circled in red.

Conceiving of y-o-u as a two-edged sales tool is a positive winner! One edge is found in the prethought verbalization that relates everything you plan to say to *you*, the customer. The other edge is the charismatic *you*. It's the you that is the product.

Your secret winning power in this one simple concept alone can put thousands of additional dollars in your annual income. No matter how good you are now, there is absolutely no limit to the expanding of this highly significant y-o-u sales tool.

Appreciate the Effect of Certain Words

Recently I read an article about the Nobel-Prize-winning author, Isaac Bashevis Singer. During his normal day he spends two hours on thinking before two hours of writing. Afterwards he devotes two hours to planning. His product is words and ideas. Winning, be it a Nobel Prize or exceptional achievement in selling, has the same ingredients.

Examining your presentation would probably show that at least 50 percent is words—your words. Every word is powering or weakening, impelling or negating, selling or losing.

There's only one way to go: Find and use those most impelling verbal ideas, with the right, powered words, to accompany your visual aids.

Thinking Is the Only Way You Achieve It

There is no short cut. Turning a problem over and over, inspecting every facet, lets your imagination work out solutions. Here are five sure ways for finding impelling verbal ideas:

1. Seek reliable evidence of customer problems.
2. Write down a list of ideas and words that relate to those problems.
3. Use Roget's College Thesaurus to check synonyms for a better word.
4. Edit your list to fit your prospect. Cross out weak words and dubious ideas.
5. Take the remaining list of verbal ideas and words and tie them into your presentation plan.

Making these five steps a part of your prepresentation system will guarantee stronger presentations with better results.

By the way, do you know any salesperson who takes the time and trouble to use a thesaurus? It's the easiest source of stronger word choices. You want to say "marvelous," but know it's an overworked word. How about "extraordinary" or "surprising"? Those came from my Roget's Thesaurus.

Different Strokes for Different Folks

In your selling, you face two totally different types of presentations:

- One-on-one, the customer and you, targeted for a *specific* order *now*. Label this a "specific" presentation.
- A group of influential people, to build a base of understanding for *future* business. Label this a "general" presentation.

Incidentally, and not in contradiction to my firm belief in solo selling, there may well be substantial support for you to use a top executive of your company to stage a general presentation. A title may command more attention and acceptance. But, don't use the title unless the exec is *great* with his or her presentation. Also, you can do some coaching in advance on the nature of the company, background of the people attending, and your sales goals at that company.

Your specific presentation:

1. Primarily a funnel—a tight, carefully planned sequence of words and exhibits that will lead to the closing of a sale.
2. Focused on one individual—his or her needs, likes and dislikes, and mood.
3. Less formal, more direct.
4. Moves quickly to a strong close.

Your general presentation:

1. Primarily to build a climate of acceptance for your company's products or services.
2. Focused on establishing a concensus from the group on how your products mesh with their needs.
3. A different response-agility is required to appraise and adjust to the reactions of several people.
4. Moves to questions and discussion.

The Impelling Verbal Ideas Are Different

Your specific presentation funnels several closing ideas toward a commitment. It is direct, congenial, logical, hard-sell. There is no doubt about your immediate objective, from your opening statement to the order-demanding conclusion.

Your general presentation uses a different language— more institutional. This doesn't mean that your general presentation should be stilted in any way. However, it is probably more formal and the words and ideas are slanted differently.

Both types of presentations are given the same verve, enthusiasm, and all-out positive salesmanship. In other words, you shouldn't low-key the general presentation to fit the hush of the Board Room. And you shouldn't be awed by titles. The bigger they are, the more understanding they are, and the more they appreciate good selling. Many of them got there via the sales route.

I am reminded of my presentation to the board of directors of a brewery. For weeks I had worked with the marketing director and the president of the company. My proposal was finally chosen to take to the board.

The marketing director insisted that my presentation be given at their board room. Repeatedly he assured me of the excellence and infallibility of his equipment. It bombed! His equipment failed. I left the board meeting humiliated, dejected, and discouraged. After weeks of work, a fine sale was lost for reasons beyond my control.

It wasn't a loss. The next morning the chairman of the board phoned with *his* idea. (He hadn't heard mine!) His *was* better. I put it together and wrapped up all the money. That shows that sometimes even a bad presentation wins.

Add Color With Idea-Language

Where slogans fit, use them. A recent market analysis from Wall Street's leading securities analyst opened with: "The dog that trots about finds a bone." That's good imagery, the kind that has a place in a presentation. Appropriate imagery adds color and light to a presentation. "A limousine liberal." "Monotonous as a metronome." "As voluble as a fox in a chicken coop." Appropriateness is the key consideration.

Alliteration can be applied to add interest to your presentation. "Powerful, persuasive presentations" sure has more impact than just "good presentations." Adding sparkle and spontaneity to your speech, is a definite device to destroy dullness. It can be overdone, but a certain amount of pleasing alliteration will provide a pulse to your presentations and a measure or two of music.

Adding a dash of seasoning keeps your presentation from becoming heavy. An occasional fitting slogan, piece of imagery, or lilting alliteration adds to the overall quality of your presentation. The inclusion of these devices, and a touch or two of humor, comes readily with your increasing expertise.

3. FIVE WINNING METHODS FOR READING, IMPROVISING, PARAPHRASING

Since your words are probably at least 50 percent of any presentation, we're going to give you some tested methods to ensure that your words provide maximum impact for your ideas.

You have made an investment in creating a presentation technique, and have carefully devised ideas and language to fit the prospect. It follows that certain methods to best present your words and thoughts protect and enhance your investment. Committing these five words to memory provides your key to winning presentations:

1. Interest
2. Flow
3. Rhythm
4. Spontaneity
5. Force

Each word keys to a method.

Hold the Prospect's Interest

Selling absolutely must be made interesting. A constant effort is applied toward fighting dullness. It is a rare presentation where, at some point, the customer isn't thinking, "I wish he'd get on with it." You want every one of your presentations to be rare. There are specific, simple, easily-applied tools to hold interest, avoid dullness.

First, you apply a *strong opening.* "*Your* idea, Jack, is the basis of this presentation." That gets his interest. From careful prior listening, you know many of Jack's ideas and beliefs. It is not at all difficult to make one of his ideas the springboard and the theme of this specific presentation. You wouldn't launch a presentation without first having a clear concept of the prospect's ideas.

If, with a new customer, you must give a presentation, without knowing his or her ideas and feelings try:

1. A brief prepresentation discussion to seek ideas that you can tie to for your strong opening and for insertion during the presentation

or

2. If for reasons of time, you must launch directly into your presentation, try to open it with a similar strength: "Your ideas, Ms. Jones, will certainly relate to many elements of this presentation. The purpose is to examine this product to find how it best fits your needs."

Observation of customers' faces, especially their eyes, will tell you whether they are with you or drifting off in their thoughts to other things they should be doing instead of listening to you. Your pace adjusts to the reception. However, you shouldn't gloss over any key sales points just because the customer is fidgeting. Your personality brightens and adjusts to gain closer interest. Also, your six-way voice mechanism goes to work to keep the presentation vibrant.

Keep a Meaningful Flow

The flow of your presentation comes from the way you tie the pieces together. This sets up your funnel leading most directly to the order.

A positive flow-director is anticipation. You know what is coming up on the next slide or card and you segue into it with: "To further illustrate," "In support of," "You see here the result."

A negative flow-director is uncertainty. This causes your customer to wonder if you know what is coming up. It may throw a wet blanket of skepticism over your entire presentation. "And, uh . . .," "And here now . . ." or "Next we have . . ."

Your flow-connectors improve with rehearsal. It takes time and thought to build and improve the smoothness that ties your presentation together. Even the spellbinder who abhors advance preparation loses believability when a slide pops up and he or she exclaims a surprised, "Whoops!"

Every successive part of a persuasive presentation ties in

with the parts preceding and following. Your flow-phrases build it all into a strong, sales-closing unity. Should any part disrupt the flow, try to find a better place in the sequence for that part or, that failing, discard it.

Flow fits all selling. All selling is a presentation.

Recently in New York, I wandered into Saks Fifth Avenue. Near that entrance was their Men's Shoe Salon. The location is strategic because men do "wander in" and shoes do hold a strong allure. Do you think they spray that smell of leather into the air as an extra enticement?

The salesman approached with a cheerful manner, glanced at my attire and my shoes, and came right to the point. "Come," he motioned, smiling, and pointed to a pair of shoes. "These will look fine on you. Let's see, your size is . . .?"

"Nine D," I replied, realizing I was committing myself.

"Let's try these." He gestured for me to sit. I complied.

"The fit is like a glove," he said. It was. I strode about feeling the amazing comfort of the new shoe. "Italian workmanship. The best," he added. "They go very well with your suit. It's a good color for you."

"Well," I mumbled. I'd had no intention of buying a pair of shoes.

"They're perfect for you," he smiled, "and today we have a 20 percent discount." He raised his eyebrows and spread his hands. "A fine value."

I walked to the mirror again. They did look good. And my wife wouldn't consider me foolish with that bargain of 20 percent off. "Yes, I'll take them. I'll wear them," I heard myself saying.

Back on Fifth Avenue, I walked along, occasionally glancing down at my new shoes. Then suddenly I thought about the simple flow of that shoe salesman's presentation:

Opening: They will look fine on *you.*
Leading: Inquiry about my shoe size.
Reason why: Fit, quality.
More reason why: Perfect for *you;* good color for *you.*
Close: Discount price. Fine value.

There were no "and, uhs," no "furthermore," no "also." It was a clean, quick, flowing presentation. Surprisingly, I had tried on only one pair of shoes, the pair that he had instantly perceived would appeal to me.

I looked down at my new shoes and smiled. It's fun being sold with a good presentation. I still like those shoes.

Rhythm Is the Heartbeat of Your Presentation

Herb K., a former IBM executive, told me how Thomas Watson, the founder of IBM, emphasized the need for rhythm in a presentation.

In music, rhythm is a fixed system. A 4-4 rhythm is four beats to the measure, the fox trot; 3-4 rhythm is three beats to the measure, the waltz. And within the measure, the beats—four quarter notes—are often broken up into eighth or sixteenth notes or stretched into two halves or one whole note. There are also rests—pauses—within measures.

In your presentation technique, the overall rhythm is more of a "feel" than anything as rigid as the form of music. The rhythm of the presentation grows with your rehearsal and application of the presentation. Actually, the growth of your feel for rhythm is an intuitive utilization of the musical form. Here's an example:

"This is winning"—Four beats to a measure.

Then "W-I-N-N-I-N-G"—The one word stretched to a full measure.

Then fast—*allegro* in music—"You've got to work at it to build the full vital force of winning." That's sixteen beats in the same span of time as the preceding one word "winning."

Then rest-rest (two-beat pause)—"That's it." Two beats, that fills out the four-beat measure.

The above example might come off as being oratorical, but it serves to illustrate that the application of the structure of musical rhythm is precisely what puts rhythm into a presentation. A perfected presentation has the rhythm of a musical composition. Listen to Paul Harvey's presentation of the news. It's rhythm all the way to the pause preceding his clipped "Good Day."

How long to pause to let a key idea sink in? Judgment,

feel. Why does the composer give a one-beat rest (pause) instead of a two-beat rest? It is important. Watson knew it. My eldest son is a screen writer. Frequently he inserts in dialogue "one beat," indicating a pause, or "two beats" for a longer pause.

Rhythm in your presentation should be natural and without affectation. Your attention to it will make it happen. The presentation feels right and paces right as rhythm comes into it.

Spontaneity Gives Each Presentation a Freshness

In live theater, an actress's unexpected deviation from the script, with a fitting ad lib, perks the actor and brightens his response. What the audience sees is pleasing spontaneity.

Your spontaneity in giving your presentations derives largely from appropriate references, which you drop in to relate elements of your presentation more directly to the customer and the product. Spontaneity also results from clever paraphrasing. To demonstrate: A slide says "Sixty-eight percent of our business is renewals." You paraphrase: "Satisfied customers—our primary objective." Your words complement the words on the slide and fill about the same span of time as it takes for your viewers to read the words.

Paraphrasing keeps *you* projected into the presentation. It obviates your reading of the actual words on the screen, or standing silent while the words are read by your customers. Also, paraphrasing ties your expression regarding the message on one slide into the upcoming slide.

Whether you use slides, a booklet, or live props, paraphrasing ties it all together and keeps a freshness, interest, and spontaneity in your presentation. *You* are the product. A robot can flip cards, slides can be automatically projected. Appropriate paraphrasing enables you to make the presentation your own personalized sales tool.

Force Is the Power Leading to the Close

The best presentations are forceful. They aren't intended to tell a story or just recite a string of facts or ideas. You've a sequence of cogent points presented with forceful enthusiasm, forceful gestures, and forceful paraphrasing. The objective with a specific presentation is to get the order; with a general presentation, to forge the acceptance of your products, your services, or your company.

Indecision is the enemy. It is true that many prospects fear decisions. Progress comes from action-commitment. The force of your logic overcomes the fear that postpones commitments. Any weakness, equivocation, or uncertainty in a presentation feeds that lurking fear of decisions.

The positive power of assured force will convert your presentations into thousands of dollars of additional income.

4. LEARN NEW CONCEPTS FOR USING DRAMA AND STAGING

Stagecraft is basic to all good presentations. Stagecraft and drama are first-class and in good taste, not flamboyant or ostentatious.

The *specific*, one-on-one presentation is best staged simply in the customer's office. Often one or more clever devices are needed to add drama within an undramatic utilitarian office. The rhinestones on the black velvet pad, pick-out-the-diamond device illustrates perception of value. Maybe set a dollar bill on fire to dramatize waste—the waste to be prevented through buying what you are about to present.

Certain *appropriate* devices can be effectively employed to add drama or surprise, to drive home a key point, or to stage a break in your presentation.

Another good showmanship technique is to weave in customer participation with your planned questions, perhaps preceding parts of the presentation with especially strong answers.

One salesperson I knew used magic. He was a really good magician. The trouble was that his magic overwhelmed his presentation.

A paper clip—just a piece of bent wire—serves well to demonstrate the value and utility of a very simple idea. Good specific-presentation selling can benefit from the added showmanship of such illustrative devices.

Different Showmanship for the General Presentation

With the *general* presentation, staging in a private room has many advantages:

1. Better control
2. A relaxed, more receptive audience
3. Ample time to be thorough
4. No interruptions by phone calls or such

Control of a presentation is important. It is best for a general presentation to flow through from beginning to end without questions. This is easily handled. When everyone has arrived, you announce, "In the interest of your time, please permit me to show you our presentation in full. Questions will arise, but some of them will be answered further into the presentation. If not, we will take time to answer any of the unanswered questions afterwards. So, if you will kindly save your questions, it will enable us to save your time by giving the presentation directly, in full, and then discuss it afterwards." No one resents it. It is more efficient done this way.

Too many presentations open with something like, "Now, this is an informal presentation. Please feel free to interrupt me at any time. We want your questions . . ." Labeling it as an informal presentation derogates your effort. It really is a formal presentation. Its content deserves full, uninterrupted, undivided attention.

Flow, Rhythm, and Pace Come From No Interruptions

You're relaxed. Your paraphrasing comes easily, building a strong flow and overall rhythm. The pace builds to your powerful conclusion.

This control not only creates a superior presentation, but has the added merit of subsequent questions being mostly, "How do we best use it?" and "What does it cost?" and "What kind of a contract is called for?" Good, positive, leading questions. A fine presentation, effectively given, rarely evokes little lint-picking, negative questions.

Don't Try to Surprise Them

For some strange reason some salespersons will invite a group
of executives to a meeting without advising them in advance
that the purpose is to give a presentation. Or they may disguise
it as a "little pitch" or "brief story" or something negatively
apologetic.

George W., president of a highly successful company,
once called on me to solicit an important contract, saying that
he "just wanted to stop by—say hello."

He placed on my desk a handsome leather folder with my
name embossed on it. "A little pitch inside," he said laughing.
I wasn't interested in a "little pitch." I wanted a forthright big
pitch. The George W. Company was on the wane, and subsequently disappeared from the scene.

Intelligent businesspeople are interested in receiving an
informative, well-conceived, and well-delivered presentation.
Likewise, astute salespersons are proud and eager to present
a compelling story. There should be no camouflaging of the
intent.

A Gentle Sales Trap

One presentation we gave, at the Rockefeller Center Luncheon
Club in New York, had an unusual outcome. At the conclusion
of the presentation our client, who was just sitting in on the
presentation, turned to our key guest and demanded, "Why
isn't that X account active anymore?"

The guest replied, "Why should they be? They're a
monopoly, and the advertising director retires in six months."

A picture germinated in my mind several days later: A
wealthy company . . . an ad director with no advertising . . . a
clean desk. Only ego could motivate any advertising.

Their former advertising had won awards. It was truly
outstanding. I had about ten of our radio stations, geographi-
cally dispersed around the country, write letters compliment-
ing the former advertising and expressing hope that it might
return.

It did. The ego responded. Within three weeks a nice

radio campaign was announced by the advertising agency. I am still wondering if anyone at the advertising agency knew that a demanding outburst after a presentation initiated a heretofore unintended radio advertising campaign.

5. BUILD STRONG SYSTEMS FOR ADAPTING AND REHEARSING PRESENTATIONS TO BEST FIT YOUR PROSPECT

There are no perfect presentations for all prospects. That's why we favor a flexible medium. Canned presentations, on film or tape, are locked in. They are not malleable. As a result they may rapidly lose their utility. The slide or card presentation is highly efficient because the material can be shifted about, parts discarded, new parts added, so it is up-to-date, and can be molded to each customer's interest.

It Takes a Lot of Work and Thought

Converting others to your point of view doesn't come easily. Every element of your presentation must be carefully related to everything you know about your customer and his or her business. Your presentation is loaded with *the customer's* ideas. Here are the ten elements to guarantee a star performance:

1. *Knowledge.* Know every element thoroughly. Be a perfectionist, an expert.
2. *Preparation.* Sequence the presentation so that each element focuses on *the customer's* needs and concepts, and relates to *the customer's* prejudices.
3. *Rehearsal.* Rehearse. And then rehearse some more.
4. *Paraphrase.* Tie it together. Relate each element to what precedes and what follows. Make it flow.
5. *Gestures.* Find the gestures that fit you comfortably and implement the flow.
6. *Sparkle.* Work in a dash or two of appropriate humor, create some alliteration, find good power-packed words.
7. *Funnel.* Each thought, each fact, every part of your presentation is designed to funnel to a sale.

8. *Tightening.* Remove elements that are not strongly pertinent to the prospect.

9. *Rhythm.* Rehearse some more to get the feel of the rhythm in the entire presentation.

10. *You.* Relate to the ten basics of Chapter One: Face, eyes, eloquence, voice, enthusiasm, gestures, empathy, attire, listening, confidence. Use a mirror.

It's work. A ton of it. But the rewards are substantial. Not everyone is able or willing to do what it takes to achieve that starring status in building a winning edge in selling.

Dramatic Presentations Open Up Infinite Opportunity

The consistent utilization of the presentation as a sales weapon will accelerate your proficiency beyond belief. Dividends in your personal stature open the way for bigger future opportunities. Personal satisfaction grows, too, with your application of the creative use of presentations. This isn't theory; it's proven, hard-cash facts.

Some Words of Creative Caution

1. Developing and rehearsing the presentation is homework. It cannot occupy selling hours.

2. Don't permit stagecraft to overpower selling. The objective is the sale, with that funnel ever clearly in mind.

3. Expect accidents and be prepared.

A Funny Thing Happened . . .

It was a large industry gathering. Part of the program called for a slide presentation from a network promotion man. A group of us were sitting nearby and watched with consternation as the promotion man dropped the slides.

Subsequently the audience rocked with laughter as the presentation began and slides showed on the screen sideways, backward and upside down.

Shortly the humiliated promotion man switched off the projector and stomped out of the hall. It wasn't really funny.

It was deplorable. It didn't have to happen. Anticipate the worst and be prepared. Rehearsed dexterity would have saved him from dismal failure.

Keep It Alive

A presentation is a living thing. It is constantly updated, altered, improved. This is essential to both its vitality and the sustained enthusiasm of the salespeople using it.

It is an axiom of good business procedure to always resuscitate a dying creative effort with a new and better effort. Usually what happens is the opposite. A highly successful presentation is considered to have done its job and is then put on the shelf and forgotten. A year or so later someone feels the vaccum and says, "Hey, we need a new presentation."

Summary

Potent presentations build your winning edge faster:

  I. By applying exciting visual techniques. Slide presentations are the most flexible medium.
 II. By discovering those verbal ideas that tip the balance: Strong, positive words, slogans, alliteration.
 II. With your mastering, reading, improvising, and paraphrasing.
 IV. By learning new concepts for drama and staging through building your strong systems.
  V. For adapting and rehearsing presentations to best fit your prospects.

It is difficult to imagine any facet of selling offering greater benefits than those gained from using fine creative presentations. They make specific sales and build company reputation. They inculcate knowledge in the sales staff, and create individual stature, which stamps you with the aura of the winning edge.

4 HOW TO WIN WITH SUPER-SMART PERCEPTIVE PROSPECTING

- Add extra dimension to your sales base
- Discover new thinking and ideas
- Open up new product applications

FIVE METHODS TO MAKE PROSPECTING INTERESTING AND PRODUCTIVE

1. Winnow out the best, the most likely

2. Use a sequential list for availability, viability, dollar potential

3. Reexamine existing customers for prospecting expanded sales

4. Build a simple system to maintain constant hot prospecting on those buying a competitive product

5. Establish your unique winning recommendation system

U nless you have a monopoly product or a service in great demand, prospecting is an indispensable facet of your successful selling technique.

Even if your product or service literally *owns* the market, the consistency, quality, and effectiveness of your winning prospecting may well determine your very survival. As an old adage says: The more backside you show up the flagpole, the more you have to lose. In this chapter we offer some winning concepts and tested techniques to make your prospecting more productive.

What perceptive prospecting will do for you:

1. Broaden the base of your business
2. Enable you to keep expanding your income
3. Open up new creative sales opportunities
4. Bring you in contact with new people
5. Expose you to new thinking
6. Uncover new product uses
7. Spotlight possible product adaptations or manufacturing opportunities

Some sales prospecting is a wheel-spin. Primarily it is judgment and experience that minimize spinning your wheels. However, there are also systems and proven methods to steer your prospecting investment towards a maximum return.

Only *Perceptive* Prospecting Pays

A costly example caused me to become more of a student of prospecting, more perceptive. We had an associate in our company with a contagious enthusiasm. When he told me about a fine prospect in Seattle whom he wished to visit, my countenance must have clouded. Seattle was about the farthest and most expensive place to go prospecting from New York.

"It's really ripe," he beamed reassuringly and added, "A sure sale!"

"But it's a long, costly flight . . . and . . . ," I mumbled, not wishing to wet-blanket his enthusiasm.

"Fly!" he exclaimed. "I never fly. I'll take the train."

My face fell. He persisted and I capitulated. The scenic trip to Seattle and back took about two weeks and a couple of thousand dollars—and no business. And subsequently, no marvelous, contagious, ebullient associate.

This early experience in building my national sales company provided me with a basic means of measuring prospecting: time, distance, money. Four keys to efficient prospecting:

1. *Organization.* A notebook exclusively for prospecting ideas and pertinent notes. The book in itself becomes a commitment to perform the extra thought and effort that prospecting requires.

2. *Planning.* Establish a regular time each week to work on your prospecting plans.

3. *Timing.* Initiate each contact most advantageously to fit your schedule.

4. *Action.* The vital key—doing it—opening up the prospect, making the appointment.

Haphazard prospecting is unproductive and time-wasting . . . unless lightning strikes in a bottle. The four keys set up your system. It's a plan that works. It ensures profitable prospecting. Thinking about new prospects becomes a habitual part of your business. Of course, prospecting is never allowed to interfere with current available business. That direct line to an order is primary.

Prospecting Also Works in Your Subconscious

A sale made relates to a certain prospect. You note it. An idea strikes you at 3 a.m. You note it. Something an associate, a customer, or a friend says fits a prospect situation. You note it. Thinking about new prospects keeps your mind tuned and receptive to ideas, situations, and people that tie into a certain prospect.

Turn Prospect Targets About in Your Imagination

Imagination differs from thinking. It delves deeper into any given prospect situation. You put yourself in the prospect's shoes. You imagine what his or her reactions might be to your proposal about acquiring your product. You also imagine his or her objections. Your imagination subsequently expands to how, why, and when to best fit product to prospect.

Effective prospecting is innovation. *Organization* of the results of your thinking and imagination keeps it all intact and in place for further reference. Divide the organization notebook into three sections:

1. *Hot Prospects.* These are the ones using a competitive product—or with an urgent need for your product.

2. *Cold Prospects.* Those which you believe or suspect should need your product. You want to get to these when it best fits your schedule. Cold prospects can haunt you when suddenly one you intended to get to makes a large purchase from a competitor.

3. *Recommendation* tie-ins.

With both hot and cold prospects, protect yourself from that lost sale out of the blue. Your company or product advertising is intended to support you with a broad awareness on the part of prospects. Reprints of ads, with an "In case you missed it" note are worthwhile. Keep your name, your product, your company in front of all prospects, hot and cold, with appropriate frequency. It is something brief, pertinent, and informative.

Creating a People Web

Ask your good customers who they know at X or Y company on your prospect list. Then note it in your recommendation system. Cross-note it under the prospect's company name.

On occasions when you have an especially elated customer, ask at that moment, "Will you please tell that to Fred Holmes?" It works. People work for you. They'll warm up cold prospects. Through your organization method you will enable them to broaden the base of your business.

1. WINNOW OUT THE BEST—THE MOST LIKELY

With some products or services almost everyone is a prospect. In that case there's no time for winnowing. You start at one end of the street and knock on every door, or stop at every store. Judgment and knowledge steers you in evaluating your best prospecting targets. Consultation with a sales manager or a sales associate adds input to your measure of each prospect's proportionate value.

For many years in the broadcasting business, the Boston territory was covered out of New York. On making the first trip into that territory, I was astonished. Everyone responded eagerly. Hot, ready-to-buy prospects were everywhere. But strangely, the subsequent follow-up provided very slim pickings. It took a long time before it finally became apparent that the enthusiastic reception was more courtesy than cash.

The Boston advertising people enjoyed and appreciated the attention from New York salespeople. They doled out prospect-like encouragement to keep bringing us back to do our unproductive song and dance. We were deluded by the applause.

Don't Be Affected by Affection

It's nice to be liked. However, reciprocal personal attraction often brings inefficiency into prospecting. In any group of salespeople you will find excessive contact directed towards comfortable relationships. It may sound crass and unappreciative of that great quality of human friendship, but I urge you to derive your maximum warmth from the humanity of prospects who respond with sizable orders. The ultimate secret of success in prospecting is found in your judgment of where to invest your selling most profitably.

2. USE A SEQUENTIAL LIST FOR AVAILABILITY, VIABILITY, DOLLAR POTENTIAL

Rank prospects in order of:

    1. Location in relationship to your other calls.

2. Evidence, or your intuitive hunch, of the viability of the prospect.

3. Best timing in relation to seasonal buying or certain other meaningful developments.

4. Dollar potential estimates.

Weighing these four factors will enable you to establish your prospecting priorities on the two lists—"Hot Prospects" and "Cold Prospects." The list is a discipline. It's there to be done. Identifying your number one prospect exacts a commitment. And so on down your lists.

3. REEXAMINE EXISTING CUSTOMERS FOR PROSPECTING EXPANDED SALES

It's so simple that it's easily overlooked.

- The contact is established.
- You have the entree.
- They are already sold.

This existing customer may be your best hot prospect.

- How can they benefit from more of my product?
- Is there an additional use for my product?
- Can there be a discount advantage?

Two problems loom before us in prospecting existing customers:

1. The tendency to put to bed the already sold client.
2. The glory of cracking a new account.

A competitor of ours was one of the best solicitors in the business. He was so good that the accomplishment of getting new clients preempted an excessive amount of his sales effort. Securing an exclusive contract to represent a choice, highly-rated, and prestigious client was a plum. He plucked quite a few plums and achieved some glory, favorable publicity, and considerable revenue.

But as is often the case, the expiration of the honeymoon with a new client lapsed into a feeling of neglect. One of our astute guys suggested, "One hundred thousand dollars added to a current client is better revenue than a one hundred thousand dollar new client." He paused. "Right?" We nodded agreement and he continued, "While their effort is concentrated on new clients, we'll put our effort into new business for our present clients. Later the neglected clients will be attracted to our company based upon a superior selling performance for our customers."

It proved to be a good simple plan. We slowed our prospecting pursuit almost to a halt and concentrated virtually all of our thinking and drive to prospecting new business for current clients.

That approach with inverted prospecting paved the way for some six-figure personal incomes. Furthermore, it created a recommendation system through which many of our best prospects came to us.

Let me hasten to suggest here the full appreciation of so-called transom business. There's more personal glory in the sale resulting from a specific creative effort. However, the business which seems to flow in effortlessly is often actually the result of doing a lot of things right in the past.

The fertilization of our imaginations was an automatic by-product of our plan. It took an abundance of imagination to springboard the creative ideas and creative selling to build substantial new revenue from existing customers. This focus of imagination expanded into creative planning for subsequent new customers, enabling us to dramatically increase their business. It is this kind of strategy, coupled with action, that adds a different slant to prospecting. Performing with exceptional excellence for existing customers is the best kind of prospecting. The words gets out.

There's Still a Time for Cold Prospecting

Inevitably one prospect on your list appears more potentially fruitful than another. That one is the number-one target. Remember, we wish to avoid wheel-spins of wasted effort. With some products, the list of real prospects might be only a couple of dozen. With other types of products or services, genuine prospects will run into the hundreds. It is not easy to sequence a meaningful prospect list. If you've ever sold door-to-door, you understand the problem. You never know behind which door lies the next sale.

Because of these prospecting differences with products and services, it is difficult to generalize on the most efficient way for all salespersons to set up the system. Suffice it to say: Virtually all good selling requires prospecting with a well-organized method to make it function most efficiently.

4. BUILD A SIMPLE SYSTEM TO MAINTAIN CONSTANT HOT PROSPECTING ON THOSE BUYING A COMPETITIVE PRODUCT

These are readily defined. However, they may be the most difficult to persuade. Hardly anyone easily admits that he or she made a bad buy—or could have made a better buy. Usually this switch-selling is long term.

Five ways to make the switch-sale:

1. First establish a rapport. In the final consideration the customer will buy from you only if he *wants* to buy from you.

2. Feed your strong factual advantages gradually. A full-blown, devastating, factual pitch may make the prospect look foolish because of the previous buying error.

3. Back up your personal calls with a gentle flow—don't overwhelm them—of supporting information and data to further enhance your product advantages. You will want to stress whatever is new and may not have been available at the time of the original decision.

4. Don't go over your contact's head. It rarely works. If forced to buy your product, he or she has lost prestige in the company and will probably resent it deeply—to your ultimate detriment. Many sales managers make grievous errors in this regard. It is natural for sales managers to urge salespersons to "go to the top."

5. One more "don't." (I wouldn't bring it up if it didn't happen so often.) Don't ever admit that the competitive purchase was a "good buy." Of course, you wouldn't knock it openly. However, when the customer says shrewdly, "Well . . . you have to admit I didn't really

make too bad a buy. Did I? Huh?" That's the time to smile, look him or her directly in the eyes, and softly state one more compelling advantage of your product.

This is an important nuance. So often one sees the salesperson's intuitive empathy cause the foot-in-the-mouth utterance, "No, not really a bad buy, but . . ." The balance just got tipped the wrong way! His or her original buying judgment has been approved by the salesperson, now a good agreeable "Joe," with no order and dim prospects from this buyer.

The foregoing five ways to make a switch-sale are, of course, only good basics. But they are the kinds of basics that often get overlooked in the fray of daily selling. A switch-sale is often a delicate negotiation that takes time and patience and considerable tact.

There are those who disagree with the foregoing approach. They believe "If you're right, hit it hard. Go for the jugular. If customers are too dumb to see it, forget it. Cross them off." You've heard that I'm sure. It's not my brand of selling. Gentle, perseverant persuasion is preferable. We've all indulged in the opposite, when circumstances justified it. I still see myself standing aggressively across the desk from prospect Perry S. and repeatedly jabbing a pen at him, saying, "Sign it!" It was a switch pitch.

He kept shaking his head, "I'm not going to sign it."

I repeated "Sign it," pointing to the contract in front of him.

"Not until I talk to them."

"Sign it!"

It went on for a couple of hours. Finally Perry signed it. However, going in I felt confident that he would sign the contract, but that he wanted me to push him hard. It's the feeling, the judgment, the type of personality involved that makes exceptions to all rules.

Keeping good customers is not to be overlooked in the prospecting effort. It is good to remember that while you are persuading prospect A to switch to your product, it is altogether possible that one of your competitors is sitting with your best customer urging him or her to switch. As a matter of policy, it is best to believe it *is* happening. The point is: Switch, but don't get switched.

5. ESTABLISH YOUR UNIQUE WINNING RECOMMENDATION SYSTEM

Getting an assist—a helping hand or a kind word—is eagerly sought frequently by everyone in business. It's a two-way street: getting and giving. There are those, of course, who only *use* other people. We'll forget about them.

Most people, except for competitors, want to help another person. This is especially true for exceptional salespersons. Why should that be? It's logical, because exceptional salespersons have an ingrained *giving* approach in all of their selling. Their customers are usually very willing, even eager to help them. There is a ripe area of opportunity here for you to build a most unique people-chain into your selling.

One of the finest developments in all of Florida thrives due to a people-chain effect. Over 75 percent of its new purchasers of homes, condominiums, or lots come from referrals.

William J., a remarkably successful automobile dealer, has a super-simple system. As he explains it, "Our concept is that *every* car we sell is an emissary out there to sell another car. Our attitude is focused to apply unusual attention, follow-up, and service to convert each sale into two sales. It works. We see to it that we have a constantly increasing number of friends out there selling for us."

As a key to your prospecting success, convince yourself of this—and prepare the necessary groundwork: that each of your current customers, and every subsequent new customer, is a key to opening up a prospect. Some of this will occur automatically because of your ability and service. Much more will come to you by building your recommendation system with careful planning.

Last night I sat talking with my son, Spencer, about the subject of prospecting. We agreed that it is absolutely essential. But it can be a gloomy, lonely, unappealing subject of the salesperson's area of responsibility.

"Maybe," Spence said with a twinkle in his eye, "you

should have labeled this chapter: Having the guts to walk through a door."

"Yes," I nodded, "it does involve the fundamental fear of all selling—the fear of rejection."

Spence said, "It has to be done. And doing it builds a vital extra something into you. It builds character. After you've made a successful prospecting call, you feel good."

I thought about my personal prospecting—the good and the bad. I thought about people who used the opportunity of unusual prospecting organization to springboard themselves to rare levels of achievement and income. I thought about one man who was assigned nothing but prospects in our company. He created a lot of business where prior to his prospecting none existed. Today he is president of his own successful company.

One of my friends, Jack C., is an exceptional entrepreneur. Among other things, he currently builds office buildings. He enjoys talking about selling and he has hired and trained hundreds of salespersons. The other day I asked him, "What makes the difference?"

Jack shifted the cigar in his mouth and squinted at me shrewdly as he replied, "*The incremental effort.* That's what makes the difference."

In all of your winning with super-smart perceptive prospecting, the following three keys, possibly more than all the rest, will ensure your adding large personal income gains:

1. Guts and ambition.
2. Perceptual planning.
3. Incremental effort

Summary

You'll build a strong winning edge in prospecting by:

   I. Winnowing out the most likely prospects.
  II. Using a sequential list for contact.
 III. Reexamining existing customers for expanded sales.
 IV. Building the system to invest your hot prospecting on those using a competitive product.
  V. Establishing and working your unique recommendation system.

5 WINNING EXTRA SALES WITH YOUR PEN POWER

- Expand a potent selling weapon in your arsenal
- Gain more competitive advantage
- Add greater depth to your selling
- Broaden your contact base

YOUR SPECIAL SYSTEM
FOR PROFITABLE USE
OF YOUR PEN

1. Reinforce your key points
2. Express appreciation
3. Promote new thoughts
4. Use preselling for the future
5. Inform about trends, industry, competition
6. Polish the apples

The strong extra dimension of frequent, brief and interesting written words from you will vastly expand your influence and your income.

Words. That's your basic tool kit. Spoken words ... articulateness ... presentation words ... written words on slides, cards, signs.

How to draw up your powerful action plan by means of written words is demonstrated in this chapter. Achieving extra skill with the pen opens up expanded income opportunities. Developing your pen as an increasingly valuable sales tool will evolve from appreciation of the proven winning techniques described on these pages. It's simple and practical, and it works.

We All Inherit Word Style

The utilization of words varies with individuals. It comes from family background, personality, and early training. A family with a tradition of abundant discourse around the dinner table creates verbalizers. Tending towards privacy, books and reading often fosters the growth of writing ability. Speech courses, participating in debates, and various sales training courses also build facility with verbal language. Some people are talkers, others writers, still others mostly listeners. The well-rounded salesperson is all three.

Individuality Flows From Your Pen

Frank B., Chairman of Eastman Radio, builds his pen-power with exclusive use of green script from a felt-tipped pen. The very fact that he has created a distinguishing personalized trademark in green ink leads Frank to use the pen more frequently as an effective, informative, and motivational instrument.

Bill B., President of Eastman Radio, adds punch with his pen by means of dramatic eye-catching devices:

> Eastman builds salespeople. The best in the
>   business!!!
> Never say die. Andrew Jackson said one person
>   with desire is a majority.
> Think big!! Sell big!! Be big!! Too few
>   salespeople think big enough.
> Hard work and a positive mental attitude—the
>   fundamentals of success.
> U—You/best . . . I/worst. Never forget *you* is
>   the best word in selling.
> Sell at the top. Don't take no from a person
>   who can't say yes.
> Integrity—It's the mark of maturity. The winners
>   of the world all have integrity.
> Ask for the order. That's the most basic of
>   selling fundamentals.
> Start early. "Don't sleep too much or you'll
>   wake up a failure."
> Make friends. People enjoy doing business with
>   people they like.
> The ingredients of E-N-T-H-U-S-I-A-S-M!

This word technique enhances Bill's winning percentages and his constantly growing income. It's an especially graphic use of the pen.

1. REINFORCE YOUR KEY POINTS

Achieve more sales with five simple reinforcement axioms:

    A.   Fill in something left unsaid.

    B.   Follow up.

    C.   Give more facts.

    D.   Feed in additional ideas.

    E.   Emphasize extra customer advantages.

This strong five-point reinforcement approach is a positive winner. It is simple, fast, and effective. There's no patent on it. It's yours.

A Second Chance to Say What You Meant to

Rarely do you leave a sales call without thinking about something pertinent you wished you had said. Invariably it is significant to the pending sale. To get the results you are after, you repair the void quickly. As soon as you return to the office, you get off a brief note such as:

"My apologies! I meant to tell you: We can *deliver immediately*. Faster implementation of savings and other efficiencies."

Fill That Waiting Period Void

Another type of brief follow-up note serves the purpose of adding emphasis. It's telling the customer what you told him or her.

"Not only will you realize major savings, but increased productivity, too. A nice combination. Will call you soon for another appointment."

Your two key advantages—savings and increased productivity—are simply reiterated. It's extra sales insurance. You can't take it for granted that your basic advantages will stick firmly in the prospect's mind. A competitor has been in the customer's office in the interim, probably expressing advantages to erase some of the luster of yours. But you take the trouble of a reinforcing note, the other salesperson may not bother. It's a simple, but often overlooked, reminder that adds to your winning edge.

Keep Your Contact Alive

Words on paper—entering the prospect's mind through the eyes—positively increase the retention of your sales points. Your note may even linger on the prospect's desk for a day or two, adding to its penetration.

The important thing is: *You did it*. You may be sure that all of your competitors won't. The balance, therefore, tips in your favor.

More facts are fed in to reinforce your key points. You rarely squander all of your ammunition in a first contact. There are always some facts in reserve for written follow-up plus emphasis. The statement of a strong fact in a quick, handwritten note builds your case. This pen technique doesn't exhaust the value of a certain fact, because you restate it in a different way, or context, on your next call on the prospect.

Feed in Extra Ideas

Additional ideas will occur to you as you think about this prospect.

> "Here's another idea, Fred. Those vehicles could be painted with red, white, and blue stripes—moving billboards for your American Brands."

It shows that you're thinking about the customer's needs. Ideas are interesting, even the ones that don't fit perfectly. Remember, there's no such thing as a foolish idea. Only the lack of an idea is foolish! Extra customer gains will inevitably occur to you as you review the sales call.

> "There's a big extra plus, Fred, in the fuel savings with this fleet. You should gain about 8 percent—a truly substantial savings over a year."

Emphasizing Customer Gains Keeps Your Thumb on the Scale

It's obvious from observing his lifestyle that Casey T. makes a comfortable income from his manufacturing business. One of his favorite sales basics is, "Keep your thumb on the scale." His allusion to the butcher's method of cheating is in no way intended to encourage any lack of integrity. To the contrary, it means: Use everything available to you to keep the balance tipped in your favor.

Reinforcing your key points with brief follow-up notes is just one way of many to keep your thumb on the scale. It evinces your keen and sincere interest.

2. EXPRESS APPRECIATION

"Thank you!" continues to be one of the most obvious, one of the most neglected, and one of the most beneficial phrases in selling. Strange—perhaps false pride resists being humble or seeming obsequious. But, "Hey thanks, thanks a million. Sure appreciate it!" can only add a plus to any successful sales situation.

The pen is a stronger way to express thanks. Lee L. is a highly competent advertising man. His substantial remuneration over a span of many years stems from superb organizational systems. No transaction of Lee's is ever completed without a personal thank-you note.

Personally Penned Appreciation is Golden

Some salespersons and companies use a thank-you form. It's impersonal and used only because the form helps to avoid the frequent oversight of this simple, friendly, essential business courtesy. No individual or company should ever get so big as to neglect expressing appreciation—*always*. Again, it cannot be overemphasized, your winning edge in selling comes more from doing a lot of seemingly little things right, than from great bursts of genius. The faithful attention to a myriad of little things *is genius*.

Penning a Back-Pat

Lee L., in his special rare style, often carried his expression of appreciation a significant step further. In his contacts he took pains to know various levels of people. Frequently, in addition to his thank-you note to the buyer, he wrote a note to the buyer's boss, which included a compliment to the buyer. Sure, the good-business, good-selling, good-public-relations intent is apparent, but that's all right. May all your competitors be dubious about using such friendly leverage while you scatter these business courtesies about with great constancy.

Pen Power for Remembrances

George W., a highly successful liquor distributor, used the expression of appreciation through the pen to a high degree of effectiveness with his sixty salespersons.

As George puts it, "Liquor is liquor. Anyone can sell by cutting the price—and the profit. We wrote a lot of catchy slogans to motivate the salespeople and the customers. Also, each salesperson had a special book in which he or she recorded birthdays, anniversaries, names of children, hobbies—everything about the customer.

"Our brands of liquor were the same as every competitor. Therefore, we had to seek a system of advantage and use it better than any competitor. The power of the pen worked for us through a constant remembering of occasions important to the customer. Our people were constantly sending out cards and notes that were thoughtful and appreciated by their customers.

"Not original, but we did it religiously, and it gave us a big edge. By the way," George chuckled, "how many people remembered your last birthday or anniversary?"

3. PROMOTE NEW THOUGHTS

An abundance of new thoughts is always available just for the effort of thinking on any pending transaction. A well-timed flow of notes across the prospect's desk keeps you there when your competitors are not there and also when your competitors are there.

How to Nag Gently With Your Pen

You needn't be too concerned about overdoing it. The opposite— underdoing it or not doing it at all—is usually the case. Normally prospects won't resent attention as much as inattention. Bill T. sometimes overdid it. He literally buried his customers in short, handwritten notes. Some griped, "Doesn't he ever run out of stuff to write?" But they bought him. Bill built a handsome income through his persistent brand of pen follow-up. It was impossible to forget him.

This steady flow of new thoughts on paper exemplifies that quality that brands the difference between plodders and get-rich salespersons. It is the never-sleeping mind that receives the flow of new thoughts to feed the brief, handwritten follow-up notes.

Some salespersons make the mistake of using the pen instead of shoe leather. Winning with your pen happens only when it is used judiciously to bridge the interval between personal contacts.

Putting Extra Imagination to Work

Ed C. uses a pad with a caricature of a man with a plant growing out of his head—"From the Fertile Mind of Ed." You've seen it. You've also seen the notepaper with a light-bulb, illustrating the bright shining idea. Or "This Is No Bull" showing a cow stepping on its over-full udder. All good, all better than "From the Desk of."

Such a pad, with a meaningful illustration, is a good reminder to use it. If your pad has an appropriate label, it can add to your individuality. How about a coat of arms with a crossed sword and pen? Or a simple $—that's the name of the game, dollars. For them, for you.

Add Impact With Penned Follow-Up

Here are five sure-fire ways to keep the follow-up sales thoughts flowing:

1. Every night, before you go to sleep, review your outstanding prospects.
2. If a thought strikes you, don't go to sleep. Get up and write it down.
3. You'll be surprised—no, startled—at how often you dream a new thought. Get up and write it down.
4. If you don't already have a suitable writing style, build a fast, friendly, interesting style to put your thoughts on paper.
5. First thing in the morning, dash off those brief notes. In the heat of the day's action you may not get to it.

Selling Is More Satisfying Than Sleeping

Frequently that dreamed idea will be so good that sleep for that night is over. Great. You'll never miss it. You won't be able to resist getting up, refining the idea, and if possible, making it your number-one call of the day.

There's power in N-E-W. It is the expression of innovation. You, as a creative salesperson, are an innovator. As such you radiate excitement. Nobody yawns when a new idea sparks the atmosphere. And when you innovate, you win.

4. USE PRESELLING FOR THE FUTURE

Harry B. is not a hot-shot executive, but he is a flourishing survivor of a vanishing breed. He is a tailor. He creates, in his shop on Third Avenue in New York, very fine men's suits, jackets, and trousers. Harry wouldn't think of himself as a salesperson, or promoter. But he does a better job of preselling than many experienced salespersons.

Every February, when the chill is frequently on Florida, Harry B. sends me two or three swatches of material with the big pitch, "Makes nice summer jackets." About ten days later, without fail, come three more swatches. "Nice slacks to go with yellow." In November come more swatches and, "Make nice Florida winter jackets."

Good, basic, effective preselling. It anticipates a need and stimulates the desire. And the timing is right.

Compelling Preselling Pen Power

It's difficult to imagine any kind of selling where preselling doesn't have a valid and valuable application. The lack of strong preselling opens a vault of opportunity. Preselling is prevalent in advertising, especially as certain products relate to the seasons, but good personalized preselling is in short supply. Its lack spotlights a rich area of extra sales impact, available for the taking.

To all things you do to create a strong winning edge, add preselling. You can do it because it's another aspect of your profession that promises to make you well-to-do faster. Good, consistent, potent preselling is a must for the winning edge.

No matter how good—and how egotistical—one is, waiting until the shoe drops before initiating any action is too big a gamble. The overly confident old pro may deride the preselling efforts of another salesperson, then demean "the lucky kid!" who gets the order. Smart old pros and smart young pros in the business of selling use preselling adroitly and consistently.

Harry B. sends swatches. Not one local clothier friend has yet taken the trouble to call me or send me a note, "Bob, I've got a summer jacket coming in next month that would look great on you." I'm ready. My wife is after me every day to get some new clothes. I'd love some local presell.

Four ways to guarantee your success in preselling:

1. Organize your knowledge of customers' and prospects' unusual buying patterns.

2. Put your idea on a calendar and tickle it sufficiently far in advance.

3. Feed our significant personally written pieces of information to create a positive attitude for your product.

4. Let each prospect and customer know that you look forward to working for him or her.

It's simple and requires little extra work, but hardly anyone is doing it thoroughly. It's a sure winner.

Penning It Keeps Preselling Flowing

My stockbroker, Lois A., is a super preseller. Hardly a day goes by that I don't receive something of interest in the mail from her, with a quick note attached. She has numerous clients, but she makes me feel that I am her only client. Lois presells with her pen to lengthen her lead among U.S. stockbrokers.

5. INFORM ABOUT TRENDS, INDUSTRY, COMPETITION

The ultimate secret of success in building your winning edge in selling is through making yourself an indispensable asset to your customers. One way to achieve that pinnacle of indispensability is through becoming a *constant, reliable,* and *interesting* source of pertinent information.

The foregoing statement is the key to the simple system that turns your informing notes into cash.

Scan to Gain an Edge

Constant. Your strong approach is supported with a predictable frequency. Your system, requiring constancy, has you alert to everything happening that relates to your customers and prospects. This involves scanning all of the appropriate trade papers, certain business publications, and the daily business section of a good newspaper. Building this into a regular habit simplifies it. If you haven't been applying this idea, it may sound like an almost impossible extra chore. It really isn't all that onerous when absorbed into a routine.

Keep Your Attitude Focused on the Pertinent

Attitude is a vital part of your becoming a fount of welcome information to your clients. It's an attitude of constant alertness. It's an attitude that slants your reading to the sources of significant information. It's an attitude that speeds your scanning of publications and enables you to quickly note, clip, or underline items that fit the interest of various customers.

Imagination expands tremendously through this approach. One thing leads to another, and ideas sprout in your mind like never before. It's a very exciting, contagious, and productive process.

Knowledge is power and your knowledge builds extensively as you utilize the constant search and dissemination of information.

Ensure Dependability From Your Pen

Reliable information is paramount. A fine company had a marvelous slogan-trademark: "The value of information is measured by its reliability." A mouthful, but a guiding light for a sales staff selling an intangible product, radio advertising. That slogan characterized the integrity of the organization. The salespersons felt obligated to live up to it.

Integrity is vital in achieving the results you want from the use of your pen. It may appear that integrity has lost some of its luster. The news is replete with stories of dishonesty in high places. The prevalence of disintegrity makes consistent integrity more uncommon and a more valuable attribute— especially in a salesperson. And especially in dispensing information to customers.

Give Your Notes a Special Flair

Interesting is what all informing notes must be. Any dullness in selling is taboo. Interesting notes call for a style, a flair, a touch of color. This is highly individualistic. However, in the absence of creative inspiration, borrow something you find in your reading. Some good, lead-in, one-liners lifted from trade papers or newspapers will add an interest and lightness and appeal in what you put out to your customers and prospects on paper.

For example, from a current business publication:

- An outside-inside view.
- Hidden treasure.
- Money talks.
- Economic intelligence.
- Coals to Newcastle.
- Not for faint heart or slow wits.
- Figure this one out.

This is not recommending plagiarism. But applying the approach used in headlines for articles and ads will provide ideas to make your pen product more interesting. For example, "Hidden treasure" might convert to "Fred, this may be a diamond in the rough." Or "Money talks" may convert to "Fred, here's an idea with bottom line possibilities."

Informing must offer value and receive empathetic reception. You don't want to write anything that gets a grunt and is crumpled into the wastebasket. Therefore, after an interesting opener, it's good to qualify: "In case you missed it" or "If this hasn't come to your attention." Give your clients the intellectual benefit of the doubt that they have scanned as much as you have. They probably haven't in most instances, but your inferred courtesy will add to the receptivity of your customers.

Keep Up With Trends

All businesses have trends. General economic ups and downs may be obvious—after they happen. Other trends are more subtle. Your product may have many advantages to assist your client to capitalize on a trend. This is where your acquired acuity from the development of a fast-scanning technique gives you a winning edge.

The trend chart at one major advertising agency showed the ascendence of television putting radio into total obsolescence. It didn't happen that way because radio adapted and competed to catch people in their cars, to inform people on the run, and to be with the busy homemaker. Knowing the right trend sold untold millions of additional radio sets and numerous transmitters and a vast array of other broadcasting equipment.

My neighbor, Tom H., was for many years chairman of a leading air-conditioning manufacturer—a highly trend-riding industry. Early in the game he created a publication called *Weather Magic*. This publication informed engineers about the way air-conditioning jobs were designed. This was the first air-conditioning manual. It became a university text on the subject. Informing with the pen in a highly technical manner paid off handsomely for Tom's fine company. *Weather Magic* not only covered trends, it set some of the trends.

To get the results you're after, make trends work for you. Many trends, observed by you, will relate directly to a use for your product. Your brief note, pointing out the tie-in, reinforces your sales.

Industry developments will on occasion trigger an idea for a note to certain customers or prospects. Changes in your industry or in the prospect's industry can frequently be used to add merit to your presentation.

Information on the client's competitors—such as new products, new methods, new promotion—with a "Did you see?" reference can be beneficial pen-selling. But only when the information adds reason-why to your sale. You can't afford to exert this extra selling effort to just be accommodating. It's all directed at conversion to cash.

6. POLISH THE APPLES

John B. was my employer for several years. An astute businessperson, he taught me an abundance of valuable lessons and concepts. John retired a wealthy man. His fine sense of business and ready sense of humor persist.

On one occasion John and I were discussing a certain employee. This man, in my opinion, was devoting too much time to pleasing the boss. John said, "Oh, Bob, I know he's polishing apples—but at least he takes the trouble to polish apples. That's more than some do."

My outlook on apple-polishing shifted somewhat. Extra effort exerted to ingratiating oneself is all part of achieving the winning edge in selling. However, your good judgment draws the line between that which is genuine thoughtfulness and that which is obvious fawning.

One of the most effective apple-polishers was Dick K. As sales manager of a major 50,000-watt radio station, Dick was master of the brief, well-expressed motivational note. It was great apple-polishing. Always helpful, contributing, and congratulatory, Dick extracted much more selling from each of his representative salespersons. His business soared.

Impress With Strong Letters

There is another kind of written selling which is both effective and unusual. This is the form letter for a group mailing. It is institutional in appeal and is intended to build a positive company image. Any salesperson with a powerful pen might use this technique in an adroit fashion and thereby carve out a unique niche for him- or herself.

My father wrote a regular letter directed to people in the publishing business. It was very well received. Therefore, I launched a similar endeavor for my company. We called these "Top Brass" letters, directed to business leaders.

It was a worthwhile sales investment giving our company a needed image. No competitor attempted to duplicate our letters to top decision-makers. We could readily feel the prestige and recognition seeping down into the buying levels. This proved to be a successful technique which tipped the balance in our favor and attracted many new clients. Following are two examples of these letters.

The Eastman Research Organization, Inc.
500 Fifth Avenue, New York, NY

For the attention of: Mr. Robert E. Eastman

Facts About Facts

An advertising agency some forty years ago had secured an important new account; made a thorough investigation of the business, its market, and its marketing problems; and was presenting its recommendations. The chairman of the board, who had listened intently, had only this to say: "Gentlemen, you've got the facts and I never quarrel with the facts."

Though that was music to the ears of the agency representatives, the chairman of the board was wrong. Facts are made to be quarreled with. Indeed the whole business of advertising is the changing of the facts of today into new and different facts for tomorrow.

Most facts are volatile. Even the universe is undergoing continuous change. Someone has remarked that the only thing that is constant is change. Nowhere is the volatility, or instability, of facts more certain or more apparent than in the affairs of people and the markets they represent. And nothing can be more disastrous than to be guided blindly by the facts of yesterday in the plans and projects for tomorrow.

There are, of course, facts that never change. We call these fundamentals. Like the law of gravity or the circulation of the blood. There are others that change so slowly that the transition is scarcely apparent even over a period of years.

Up to a few years ago no fact was more firmly established than that glass is brittle. Now, here in Florida (where I happen to be writing this letter), it is hard to find any other than glass fishing rods, the last word in toughness and flexibility.

In research, the gathering of facts is essential. There can be no research without it. Still it is only the first and in some respects the least important phase of research. There are four steps, each of increasing importance. These are:

What *is* it?
Why is it?
What *of* it?
What are you going to *do* about it?

That is, (1) gathering the facts; (2) determining the reasons for the facts; (3) establishing what they mean, or interpretation; (4) deciding what needs to be done.

In our chosen field of advisory Editorial Research, we have had a great deal of experience in gathering the facts pertaining to all the various phases of the thing called readership—more than twenty years of it, preceded by years of pioneering in general market research. This is still the simplest and least challenging part of our job. There was never any great problem of gathering dependable facts; it was much more important to find out what kind of facts were needed. That took some years of doing.

It was still more important, and more difficult, to find out *why* the facts were what they were. That is still difficult. But unless you find out the reasons as well as the facts, you are getting nowhere.

Of even greater importance than these two preceding steps is *interpretation*. There is no greater fallacy than the idea that facts speak for themselves. Facts standing by themselves can sometimes be very misleading. It is so easy to jump to conclusions instead of arriving at them through patient study. It took us years to discover the significance of some things that today seem perfectly transparent.

And then comes the most important step of all, determining what needs to be done in the light of the facts and the interpretation. That's the practical side of our job, in which, of course, we are greatly aided by our years of working shoulder-to-shoulder with editors and publishers in many different fields in meeting and solving all manner of editorial and publishing problems.

Solving them all? Why no, of course not. We've both made our blunders and profited by them. And some problems are never solved. That's what makes the publishing business, and ours, so exciting.

And that's a fact!

R.O.E.

ROBERT E. EASTMAN & CO., INC.
527 MADISON AVENUE
NEW YORK, NY

The other day our sales manager, Joseph Cuff, posed a question I think may be of interest to you.

He asked, "Why use the labels of 'consumers,' 'market,' and 'masses' when what we really mean is 'people'?"

A good thought. Your customers and prospects are just plain, living, human *people*. Whether the Smiths of Boston or Joneses of Omaha, they eat, wear clothes, drive cars, catch colds.

In advertising we tend to lump them all together as a faceless, inorganic "mass market." Too often, in an insulated atmosphere of sophistication, clever phrases and secret ingredients are overworked when basically the objective should be one of telling and retelling more and more *people* in a direct and sincere manner that you have a *good product* and what it will *do for them.*

We have a slogan: "It takes people to sell people." Spot Radio on-the-air personalities have a close tie to their people. These radio personalities are better known than most Government officials.

The people love radio. Over 90 percent of them listen every week for anywhere from ten to twenty-four hours. Repeated research proves it is the people's first source for news, weather and community affairs.

The Spot Radio medium affords the personal touch, ideal for frequent contact about your product with simple, honest, hard-working *people.*

Sincerely,

Robert E. Eastman

You might call those letters one more form of apple-polishing. They proved the effort worth the investment of both time and money.

Summary

Here's how to draw up an action plan to make your pen add to your winning edge:

 I. Develop a habit of a brief note follow-up. Reinforce key points. Fill in something left unsaid.
 II. Use your selling pen to express appreciation always. "Thank you for a fine order." Thank the buyer's boss, with a pat for the buyer.
 III. Write notes to promote new thoughts. It puts you there when your competitor isn't.
 IV. Use your pen lavishly for preselling. Build relationship. Let prospects know you anticipate the pleasure of working with them.
 V. Become an indispensable source of information via penned notes. Assiduously scan publications.
 VI. Go ahead, polish the apples with the pen—judiciously, not obsequiously.

6 HOW TO CREATE ATTITUDES THAT AMPLIFY YOUR WINNING EDGE

- Selling is intertwined with attitudes
- Recognizing attitudes is essential
- Understanding attitudes enables you to work them

SIX WAYS TO GUARANTEE YOUR SUCCESS BY MAKING ATTITUDES A POTENT SALES TOOL

1. Make emotions such as fear, greed, uncertainty work for you
2. Convert errors to wins
3. Develop a healthy outlook on sickness
4. Skillfully use the studied negative
5. Develop your "just-one-client" concept
6. Learn how to be truly fabulous

An amazing technique that always works is harnessing attitudes. There's a ton of new sales power in attitudes. Focusing this extra power in specific ways will vastly expand your influence over others. Cultivating attitudes is a cash crop.

Some facets of attitude are instinctive, automatic. Certainly most salespersons make an effort to be congenial, personable, and knowledgeable. It's the bedside manner of our profession.

You Control Attitude Power

A select few of the superstars of selling take the trouble to work attitudes intensively. They discover the ways to study, analyze, and forge various attitudes into powerful, persuasive, profitable sales tools.

One of the cornerstones of this concept is knowing that attitudes are malleable. They are clay to be molded into the creative result you desire. The tangible order-producing results are limitless. No matter how adept you've become in making attitudes work for you, there is always more of the available power to be garnered.

Our entire attitudinal thrust is to convert the negative to a positive. No to yes. It's all pointed to converting others to our point of view. That's much of the essence of winning selling and winning management. They're the same thing.

No doubt the enthusiastic attitude is accepted as fundamental. We're going to approach it somewhat differently. Plain, raw, hooray enthusiasm can sometimes be counterproductive. Our approach is subtler, shrewder, and more analytical. It generates an enthusiasm that glows softly, rather than screaming from the housetops.

Everything affects attitude. The weather, the cup of coffee, the spouse's words, the night before, the boss's personality, yesterday's rejections. All the more reason why attitudes need to be harnessed positively and focused to work for you. The secret of beneficially using attitudes is found in concentrating on certain attitudes and becoming especially expert with them.

1. MAKE CERTAIN EMOTIONS WORK FOR YOU

- Fear
- Greed
- Uncertainty

Let's settle for these three potent emotions. Fear is a fantastic force. It's true that our minds are constantly full of flitting fears. The drug demoral is an effective presurgery drug because it turns off that part of the brain that fosters fear.

It's futile, impossible, and meaningless to even try to begin to enumerate most of the fears that beset us in our daily pursuit of the dollar. However, there are four specific fears which you'll want to harness to help build your sales and income.

1. The fear of contact.
2. The fear of rejection.
3. The fear of ineptitude.
4. The fear of failure.

Fear Is a Positive Force

My friend Norm G. tells me that the term "fear" is inappropriate. Possibly he is correct, he being much smarter than I. Apprehension might be a better word. To me it was *fear*. I was scared. If I didn't knock on that door and make a sale, my wife and children would not be provided for. Fear drove me, and I believe that behind many a calm, possessed, and strong exterior there is a boiling fear that fires achievement.

Therefore, I urge you to embrace fear. Welcome it as a strong ally rather than a debilitating foe. It is well known that successful performers—actors, singers—feel fear before each performance. An exhilaration follows in overcoming the fear. An actor would be more concerned if the fear were missing before a performance. By effectively harnessing the power of fear you have a new successful technique tipping the balance in your favor.

In my earliest selling—at age ten, of potato peelers door-to-door—my childish fear was basic: If I didn't sell the potato peeler, I didn't go to the Saturday movie. That urgent need led me to ring the doorbell and stutter out, "Would you like to buy a potato peeler?"

Channeling Fear Builds Confidence

A new contact, like a new audience, *should* cause stomach butterflies. You shouldn't be relaxed, casual, or unperturbed. You accept the attitude of fear, concern, discomfort. You accept these stimulants because they make you better.

You're better prepared. You don't worry about hitting the high C because you know it's your responsibility. That's the first step in harnessing the fear of contact. It's not just a matter of hyping yourself, rather it's a case of knowing that the fear is working for you. It adds to your alertness; it enhances empathy and encourages listening.

The fear isn't going to evaporate. It will and always should be there prior to each new sales contact. It is not a lack of confidence. It is confidence that you have a strong attitude under control. The fear becomes exciting, like much of the fear of the unknown.

How many—honestly—how many sales contacts have you avoided, or postponed, or rationalized away because of that lurking, unbridled fear? I'll admit to an embarrassing bunch of them. It took me many years to actually welcome the presence of fear as a positive stimulant.

One of my model sales reps was Dick B. He taught me a great deal about the nuances of good salesmanship. Therefore, I was somewhat astonished at the abject fear on his face when we were en route to the hotel to meet with our client, the world-famous U. S. senator from Oklahoma, whom we had not met previously. Perhaps it was Dick's conversion of the fear that impressed me most. His words were concise, well-stated, and informative. It was a good meeting. He converted his fear to an eloquent performance.

The fear of contact can be a major sales detriment. A highly competent salesperson will have that fear through all of his or her life—all the way from sales manager to chairman of the board. It is not forever a sales detriment to the superstar salesperson because he or she has learned to make fear of contact a stimulant that is satisfied only by knocking on that door and striding in to face that prospect.

Wally N., a former executive at Kodak, now retired in Florida, waxes enthusiastic in discussing this positive value of harnessed fear. But he cautions, "Don't confuse fear with worry. Worrying is usually a wasteful trait. Too many people worry about things they can't control."

The Fear of "No!"

Turning the fear of rejection into productive selling is an artful nuance of winning selling. Untold thousands of sales calls have not been made because of the fear of rejection. Many new ideas have been choked off at birth because of the expected rejection: "Crazy—ridiculous—foolish."

One of our charter clients was in the process of firing us. It was a crucial time for our young company. We were demoralized, angry, and full of fear. After unproductive days of anguish, we came to a very simple conclusion. We believed we had done all we could to prevent the loss of the client. Therefore, we told each other, we had to accept it. It was the client's prerogative to fire us. Someone summed it up: "We can't be in business if we can't handle losses."

That concept altered the entire course of our company. Losses—rejections—are inevitable. We determined to do our very best to avoid them. That failing, we vowed to take it in stride, seek the cause, and use it as a lesson to minimize future losses.

The point is carved in granite: *No one can achieve that winning edge in selling without an acceptance of the inevitability of rejection.*

Therefore, the normal, prevalent fear of rejection is accepted as an ingredient of all selling, all innovation, all progress. The vital aspect of harnessing this fear is never to permit it to win. Never allow it to stand in the way of making a sales call. That's a big never. There isn't a salesperson alive who doesn't harbor some guilt over those calls unmade because of fear of rejection.

Questioning Your Own Competence

Converting the fear of ineptitude to your advantage is a necessary attitude adjustment. Because you are a real pro salesperson, ineptitude rarely concerns you. But I would wager there are occasions when you are in awe of your prospect. His or her stature in the industry, reputation for exceptional astuteness, or aggressive competence at demolishing sales presentations causes you to pause and take stock.

First, consider the likelihood that some of your competitors will duck the call. That's a plus for you. Second, accept the possibility that the prospect's exceptional intellect might just happen to work to your advantage, or that, at worst, you would learn something. Third, if your presentation is utterly destroyed, you could conceivably exact a sympathetic, "Gratitude Factor" kind of response.

Case in point: Jack S., sales manager of WNEW in New York, and I visited Chicago together. Our target—a large meat packing company. We were met by a churlish, old, totally unwelcoming marketing manager. He didn't want to see us or our presentation, or have anything to do with us. Believe me, I felt inept!

The meeting had been set up by the old man's assistant. Despite our embarrassment, I sensed a potential ray of hope in the assistant's discomfort, and decided to give the presentation, come hell or high water. The old codger slept through the presentation. He actually snored. At the conclusion he mumbled his way out without so much as a handshake.

The assistant manager, openly tinged with embarrassment, invited Jack and me into his small office. Without taking the time for apologies, he said, "Fellows, I don't have much budget for New York. What can you do with $30,000?"

Turning Fear Into Dollars

What could we do! We wrapped it up—got the entire budget. Thirty thousand was a fine piece of business. It was well worth the trip and the humiliation. My fear of ineptitude at the outset converted to $4,500 of commissions in pocket.

The fear of failure is a potent sales tool that's discovered, appreciated, and applied by only a very limited few. This attitude—the fear of failure—is tremendously motivational. A smart salesperson is not afraid of this fear even if at times it seems almost paralyzing: "If I don't come up with something stronger, better, different, I'm going to lose this business! I can't lose it."

The fear of failure is a money-maker for those who have it and use it, because it sets off intensive thinking, probing, and imagining. There are always new answers.

Fearing Failure Forges Closing

Bill B. and I were breakfasting in New York when he described the prospect of a valuable new client. It was exciting to hear the course of a dramatic and highly competitive sales drive. "It hangs in the balance," Bill said, "today's the day. It's between the two companies."

"But, Bill, it would be a shame to lose it." I wanted to stimulate his fear of failure. "There surely must be more things you can do to help ensure your securing the contract. You can't just leave it in the balance. Do something—anything—to keep their minds on your company, to tip the balance in your favor."

The coffee turned cold as we brainstormed a half-dozen or so additional things which could be done before that day's decision time. "Bill," I said, "the very fact that you keep trying hard up to the last minute is bound to weigh in your favor. They won't be annoyed. To the contrary, they will be appreciative of the intensiveness of your desire to win that contract."

Bill was up out of his chair. "Hey, so long." He was off at a trot to begin implementing a bunch of simple, creative, nudging ideas. His fear of failure, enlarged by my words, set off a revived stream of sales action.

At five o'clock I phoned Bill's office. The phone exploded with a jubilant, "Hey, chief, we got it!"

It would have been easier to shrug and accept that posture of, "We've done everything possible," and let it go at that. With the contract lost, there would be the consoling, "You did your best." But no sale, no profit . . . no new cash in the pocket . . . no pride of successful achievement.

Fear Motivates to Try Harder

Once more I am reminded of Jack C's one-liner, "It's the incremental effort." The fear of failure inspires much of that powerful incremental effort.

Undoubtedly there exist many salespersons who would argue against my four fears. It would offend their pride to admit to any kind of fear. I've heard many of these fearless phonies rant about "The stupid buyer . . . our product didn't fit . . . the lousy research . . ."

Give me the salesperson who is so scared silly about losing a piece of business that he or she can't sleep. They'll win every time over the fearless braggard loaded with self-justifying excuses. The latter ought to be at least frightened a little bit that a smart sales manager would see through the bluff and invite him or her to find employment elsewhere.

Call it what you want to, I'll call it F-E-A-R!

- Fear of contact
- Fear of rejection
- Fear of ineptitude
- Fear of failure

Each strong emotion forges an attitude and action that can tip the balance in your favor. Fear is much stronger as a motivator than are worry, concern, and apprehension.

Before we leave this concept of fear as a potent sales tool, let's shift for a moment to the other side of the desk to look at a few of the fears that beset a customer.

- Fear of making a mistake
- Fear of being sold
- Fear of offending another salesperson

Your awareness of the constancy of all fears enables you to be more aware of these customer fears. Therefore, you become more sensitive to these emotions and more competent at defusing them when they come between you and a sale.

Greed Is Great

How to turn greed into cash spotlights another potentially controversial sales nuance. Greed is a much maligned and misunderstood term. Its simple, stark imperativeness gives it money-making punch.

Profits, money, greed—all are negatives in the minds of many people. It's strange in a capitalistic country that the term "obscene profits" could ever spring into the headlines. Or "unearned income," labeling the interest or dividends from hard-earned, invested, after-tax dollars. There's a negative influence attached to the aggressive pursuit of dollars.

This idealistic phoniness has no place in the outlook of the winning edge. Our objective is all the dollars you can earn—and more. What's wrong with the dollar sign as a target. Is it greedy to want to earn a hundred thousand or a million a year? If so, I'm all for greed.

Get Your Full Share Through Greed

Greed is a winning attitude. It's the attitude that keeps you from settling for too small an order. A buyer can easily brush off a salesperson who is willing to settle for a token order. Go for the whole pie—all you can justify—rather than a small slice. That is constructive greed.

In order to have greed working for you, you must be open about the fact that you earnestly—eagerly—desire all of the customer's dollars your product can ultimately warrant. There's no room for a solace slice for "Good old Joe."

A Healthy Greed Averts the Brush-Off

"Sure, I'm greedy," is admitted, "greedy to see to it that every dollar invested in my product is the best possible way you can invest your funds." Notice, we said invest, not spend.

You have to know that your customer can't hold too much respect for the salesperson who grasps at crumbs and is satisfied to walk off with a minimal order. It doesn't serve the best interests of the customer either.

It gives no pleasure to deflate the ebullience from a salesperson's new order. Nevertheless, the order needs to be evaluated. Was it enough? Did your merchandise deserve a much larger share?

Also, there is no joy and less income in being faced with the reality of having been insufficiently greedy. Wanting more, selling for more, and securing more is the only attitude that propels a salesperson into his or her goals for substantial income. I'm proud to label it greed. May most of your competitors be disdainful of greed.

Uncertainty Creates Opportunity

Control of customers through your mastery of uncertainty is a subtle technique designed to put a bunch of new dollars in your pocket. This is not theory—it is a proven money-maker.

The more complex things become in our society, the more prevalent is uncertainty. A buyer listens to multitudes of claims of various salespersons and becomes confused, lost in a maze of conflicting detail, and wavering in an uncomfortable feeling of insecurity. With your finger on the pulse of the situation, you recognize the mounting uncertainty. Appraising this common situation, you know that the customer's uncertainty is infecting your sales competition with considerable uncertainty.

I don't want to jump the gun on an upcoming chapter on the power of positiveness—which is vital to capitalizing on the widespread existence of uncertainty. However, there are some simple specific techniques that may be applied and prove very profitable to you.

Make Uncertainty Work for You

It's simple, but not easy. You must be willing to burn a lot of midnight oil to corral those extra dollars. Nowhere in this book do we say that getting rich is easy. Six ways to get sales out of uncertainty:

1. You find the opportunity to empathize with the enormity of the customer's problems.
2. All the time you personally exude an attitude of certainty that good solutions will be worked out.

3. You get on the customer's side of the desk, mentally, possibly actually.

4. You offer to assist, to do some of the work for him or her.

5. By objectively sifting the problems, you develop a plan of action for the customer.

6. You work in creative ideas which become *the customer's* ideas.

Of course, this won't always work. It entails a special effort. When it succeeds, it usually pays off substantially. The customer is thrilled with "our" plan—and you get the lion's share of the business.

Bob D. faced just such a situation. The customer wanted to put together a spot radio campaign for the product, but had no idea how to proceed. Bob stepped in helpfully and reassuringly, and he won the customer's confidence. Now he was behind the desk putting the pieces together for the customer.

Bob won a $500,000 exclusive order. It produced fine results for the product. Today, I must add, Bob is on his way to becoming very rich. The six-way plan outlined above proved a gold mine for Bob D.

Remember this, there is no way to lose from trying this technique. A sincere offer to help is always appreciated even if the customer doesn't accept your offer.

By making the emotions of fear, greed, and uncertainty work hard for you, you will establish selling processes that dramatically build your winning edge.

2. CONVERT ERRORS TO WINS

This is an essential attitude to achieving even greater success. There's a normal tendency to let a sleeping dog lie, not to be concerned about an error. It may be overlooked, or if noted, quickly forgotten. The winning-edge attitude doesn't take that chance. The odds are against it.

The Uncorrected Error Is a Lingering Blemish

The positive percentage is always in your favor when you go back to the client and openly correct the error. Think about the Watergate error that caused the President of the United States to resign. If quickly, openly, and with appropriate humility, the President had stated, "We committed a foolish mistake. We're sorry. We apologize," that would have been the end of it.

Jack H. was a competent, honest, and hard-working financial man. However, he was error-prone. His principal errors were: (1) Waiting for someone else to find his error. (2) Attempting to exonerate the error with, "It's human to err." It was repeatedly emphasized to him, "It is inhuman to err. You only err once if you step off a curb in front of a taxi." His lack of concern over errors ultimately cost him his position.

Four steps to convert errors to wins:

1. Go see the customer immediately and correct the error.
2. Use it as an opportunity to demonstrate your insistence on accuracy and integrity.
3. When possible, convert the correction into an improvement.
4. Use the resulting positive climate to try to either close or expand the sale.

Cal F. is a highly successful real estate developer in Denver. Recently he told me about one of his richest error-to-win conversions. When he was a young real estate salesman he gave a wildly wrong quotation to a very shrewd buyer. As soon as Cal became aware of his error, he hastened back to the buyer to correct it.

"I knew your quote was way off," the buyer said with a twinkle in his eye. "I wouldn't hold you to it."

Cal never sold that buyer. "But," he said, "it's a funny thing. Over the years he sent me a ton of business."

Keep the Door Open for Better Timing

Knowing when to quit is a positive means of avoiding a common error of ill-timed overpersistence. Good judgment dictates a retreat. You're up against an unbudging customer, or it's obvious there's some urgent problem on his or her mind. Exit calmly. It's time to quit and come back another day.

My long time friend, Tommy H., says "Remember, he has to want to buy you." Without a monopoly product, you normally cannot sell prospects against their will. Tommy became a millionaire through his unusual talent of getting people to want to buy him. On one occasion in particular, we had all the facts in our favor, but the client wanted to buy Tommy. We lost.

Your empathy tells you when to quit. This keeps the door open for the customer's receptivity on another day. Then you'll have a better chance that he or she wants to buy you.

Losing Skillfully Aids Later Winning

Knowing how to lose can be an important secret of your winning edge. Losing can unleash anger. Bridges get burned. You don't choose to be a good loser, but you can choose to be a smart loser—when losing is inevitable. Four keys to being a winning loser are:

1. Don't get mad.
2. Don't appear to be capitulating.
3. Leave a reasonable doubt.
4. Keep the door open.

In sports the furious loser exhibits an appropriate image. But in selling that image has virtually zero value. Many a salesperson feels obliged to do the mad-fury dance for his or her sales manager. Possibly that's intended to obviate criticism for the loss. Anger at all levels of selling is unproductive.

When the loss is apparent, some salespersons react with a hound-dog look of sadness. Perhaps they wish to evoke sympathy. There was a woman in my business who would actually cry when she lost a certain order.

"Thanks" for No Order Doesn't Fit

There is a terrible tendency in selling to be a good sport about a loss by congratulating the customer on his or her decision. "Well, Al, you made a good buy." Did you ever hear yourself saying that?

A while back, Stan C., vice president in charge of marketing of a large dishware company, read some of these winning sales concepts. He wrote me: ". . . one section—on not being a good loser—was a revelation to me, and already has paid off."

Leaving a reasonable doubt is the most effective, businesslike way to terminate a losing transaction. You say, "Please—as you use the widget—check it out carefully for its performance on cost and efficiency. I'll be back." Smile, shake hands, and leave. It's not necessary to thank someone for not buying you!

Don't Let Sleeping Losses Lie

Since losing—the opposite of winning—is and always will be an inevitable phase of all selling, it's essential that you take the positive steps to making losing work for you. As the saying goes, "So it's not a total loss." The follow-up after a lost piece of business is vital. Let your competitors turn their backs on losses. You keep feeding in those informative notes towards a future opportunity to get that business back.

Jack M. is my kind of a real estate salesperson. He puts imagination, long hours, and sagacious effort into selling millions of dollars of choice real estate each year. He says, "Always turn adversity to advantage."

Jack has a fine talent at converting objections to positives. If someone objects to "Such a small town," he counters, "It's low-profile—big towns are easily accessible." "But you have no place for my yacht." He replies, "We're midway between two inlets, and several fine marinas are nearby." The prospect says, "But it's an agricultural area." The positive from Jack, "That's good. It avoids overcrowding. The citrus pickers and the cowboys keep the city young and give it a flavor."

Jack's technique is fast-on-the-feet conversion of potential errors into wins. And win he does—a lot.

Find That Definable Degree of Difference

Zig when your competition zags. That often proves to be a very valuable technique. If, for example, you know that a principal competitor tends towards an overly detailed presentation, you make your presentation the epitome of conciseness. If a competitor usually calls on a customer in the afternoon, you get in ahead, first in the morning.

There are many strategic advantages to be gained through applying the zig-zag angle. Another facet of it is through innovation in selling techniques that make it difficult for your competition to react. If you put together a fine slide presentation, for example, it will take some time for a competitor to come up with anything to counter your special creative effort. Also, competitors are often loath to copy another competitor's plan.

Be a Willing Imitator

Mil B. is without question one of America's great business leaders, so recognized by *Fortune Magazine*'s Hall of Fame for Business Leadership. Recently a group was discussing a highly innovative and successful service being marketed by a large brokerage firm. Surprise was expressed that no competitive firm had followed the lead. One of the group said, "It's a strange thing—they all resist imitating."

Smiling and spreading his hands, Mil said, "I have always believed that if you can't come up with an improvement, go ahead and copy it. It's not patented. And it's tested."

Even though there are numerous good opportunities to zig when your competition zags, the principle is not inviolable. If a competitor is doing something especially unique and you can't better it, *steal it*. Don't let your desire for originality stand in the way.

3. A HEALTHY OUTLOOK ON SICKNESS

We used to have a slogan in my company: "Much of the world's work is done by sick people." I must admit to a strong prejudice against so-called sick days in union contracts. It is undoubtedly one thing that has caused U.S. industry to lose to some foreign companies. Here are five tested, simple remedies for sickness:

1. Don't give in to it.
2. Take a couple of aspirin.
3. Struggle to the office.

4. Don't make calls if you're sneezing.

5. Use the day constructively inside.

It's not uncommon to wake up poorly. A small amount of rationalizing can make you turn over in bed and decide that you're too sick to go to work. Even some otherwise good salespersons pamper themselves too much. Again, it's a matter of creating an attitude that builds your winning edge. On those rare occasions when you're really ill, good judgment requires staying in bed. Everyone knows the difference between an incapacitating illness and a rationalized day off.

Be Antagonistic Towards Sickness

A healthy outlook on sickness provides you with more selling time and greater earnings. Predictably, you are going to feel under the weather on many days during the next twelve months. So what do you do? You either sell less and make less money, or you recognize most of that illness as being something you can overcome. With that positive attitude shift, you get richer faster than those who lie in bed and feel sorry for themselves.

It's my contention, from observing hundreds of superb salespersons, that the ones with the healthy outlook actually are healthier. There once was a famous doctor who promoted better health by urging people to frequently repeat this statement: "Every day in every way I'm feeling better and better." That's attitudinal medicine.

Ed L. is a steadfast student of salesmanship. He became well-to-do from his fine sales talent. He never pampered himself out of a day's work. But ask him how he feels and he'll give you a recitation of ailments a yard long. Well, nobody's perfect, not even Ed. He planted one unusual health/sales thought with me. "Before you hire a man, ask him when he goes to the bathroom in the morning." Immediately my mind's eye saw certain men with the habit of going directly from the sales meeting to the men's room.

That's a tough subject to discuss. One's personal habits are private. However, I'm free to discuss it here to the extent of recommending that all personal grooming and toilet needs be taken care of before arriving at the office or embarking on your day's selling. Habits and routine are all controllable to fit your best sales needs. All it takes is an attitude that insists that your personal needs are not permitted to preempt valuable sales time.

This subject of an attitude on sickness may read like preaching. And it may have no bearing for you. However, I feel impelled to lean on it as an important successful technique. You are guaranteed more success with your sales machine by insisting on less down time. *You* control it—sickness doesn't.

4. SKILLFULLY USE THE STUDIED NEGATIVE

This is a selling nuance worth thousands of extra dollars in your pocket. The studied negative is either a simple or a complex expression of a negative on your product or service. The intent is to get the prospect to assume the positive, to your benefit. The *studied* negative is cleverly contrived. It is, indeed, a shrewd sales maneuver.

The simplest example is the enthusiastic entrance into Harry's office with a big smile and, "Hey, Harry, do I have a crazy idea for you!" After laughingly explaining your concept, you frequently elicit a positive response:

> "Hey, that's not so very crazy," or "Yeah, crazy. But interesting," or a friendly "Go peddle your crazy ideas elsewhere!"

Jack B., longtime executive with the world's largest securities firm, uses this studied negative: "Here's three stocks you *shouldn't* buy." Jack is a keen student, believer, and applier of selling nuances. And he's a self-made millionaire.

Six ways to get positive action from the studied negative:

1. Use it on the bored prospect.
2. Apply it to the prospect who fights a logical, detailed presentation.
3. Create a different approach with a frequently contacted customer.

4. Find a means to more readily make your idea become the client's idea.

5. Invite participation to disagree with you—towards your ultimate benefit.

6. Devise a selling nuance that doesn't sound overly eager.

Let me stress the word *studied*. You use it thoughtfully. Some salespersons state negatives carelessly for strange reasons. I've seen them spout a list of negatives on their product to impress their sincerity or integrity. (Or stupidity!) Others assume a negative attitude to try to intimidate.

My father, Roy O. Eastman, founder of the Eastman Research Organization, used the studied negative skillfully:

> I was asked by a prospect if I would be willing to give him the names of some of our clients as references.
>
> "To be sure," I answered. "And, of course, I'll pick our best friends and I'll probably dictate the kind of letter I'd like to have them send you. How about my telling you instead about the three clients of all we have served in the past ten years who weren't satisfied and why we fell down?"
>
> We got the order.

The studied negative is a highly useful selling nuance on certain occasions. Also, it is little understood and not overworked. It warrants one more excellent example of my father's use of the device:

> Our tongues had been hanging out for new business so long that they were dry and cracking. With a couple of my associates I was calling on a client of ours in New England who was in the pharmaceutical business. He had recently brought out a new product.
>
> "Maybe we ought to make a survey on this," the client suggested. A light of hopefulness came into my companions' eyes. It would be nice to eat again.
>
> "Well, why?" I asked, looking dubious.
>
> The client scowled and answered defensively, "There are

a lot of things we don't know and really ought to find out."

"Such as . . ." I ventured. The jaws of my hungry associates had fallen perceptively. They were watching me apprehensively.

The client went on to enumerate. He made a pretty good job of it.

"But can't you get most of that from the salesmen's reports, or the sales records?" I asked.

"No, we can't," he answered more positively. By that time, the folks with me were sure I'd gone crazy. I tried once more.

"Then how about giving the salesmen a questionnaire and seeing what they can dig up?" One of my companions suddenly sat down—to keep from falling.

The client was almost belligerent. "You know darned well the salesmen are no good as investigators."

I reluctantly capitulated. We agreed to make the survey. The client had sold himself much better than I could have sold him. And there wasn't a doubt in his mind *why* he needed the survey.

Your skillful application of the studied negative is a proven successful technique that will frequently tip the balance for you.

5. DEVELOP YOUR "JUST-ONE-CLIENT" CONCEPT

This is a special attitude for doctors, lawyers, teachers, and *especially* for salespersons. It was dramatically driven home to me on the occasion when our new client from Chicago was making his first visit to our New York office. As he was introduced to various salespersons, he made friendly comments. To one man he said, "How's business?"

The salesman was involved in a huge new campaign for several markets. He enthusiastically recounted his large orders from Indianapolis, Saint Louis, Cleveland, Pittsburgh, and Columbus. The client from Chicago frowned, "Nothing for Chicago?"

Our very next private sales meeting was on the subject:

Just-One-Client (JOC). The client from Chicago is only, and quite properly, *only* interested in business that is prospect for his market.

This attitude was cultivated with our people to such an extent that even if a client from Columbus insisted on talking about Cleveland, we'd say, "Let's get back to Columbus." It became a fetish.

The development of the JOC concept to a high degree of perfection might be designated as a top-priority attitude. That customer across the desk at the moment is the most important person in the world. You control that person by focusing your entire presentation on *him* or *her*. If he or she or talks about you, don't take the bait. Get the discussion directly back to the customer's needs and problems and how the product fits the customer and his or her company.

Get Right to Business Comfortably and Unconventionally

Early in this book I pointed out that many facets of building your winning edge fly in the face of conventional sales tactics. It's these *unconventional*, tested, and proven money-making techniques that make this book worthwhile. Your acquisition of certain new, interesting, and subtle techniques will put a valuable extra productive quality into your selling. This certainly cannot be created from simply following traditional paths.

"Whittlin' talk" is considered by many sales experts to be essential to good selling. It's conventional. You are supposed to launch a sales pitch with diverting, friendly, solicitous conversation: "How's Marie?" "How are Freddie and Joan? Doing well in school?" "Your back okay now?" "Got that handicap down to an eight yet?" Remember, almost all of the conventional salespersons ply that customer with conventional "whittlin' talk."

By banning this preamble from your selling, you will make more sales, expand your selling time, and gain added respect. Launching directly into the *you*, the product—and business success for the client—becomes the thrust of your presentation. It's the *one* client—and what you bring to him or her of value. Your efficient, friendly, and businesslike approach is appreciated by the customer.

Time-consuming "whittlin' talk" becomes unessential in your selling because of your consistent application of the Just-One-Client concept. Your personal thoughtfulness is of birthdays and anniversaries; remembrances become more meaningful if you eliminate family, hobbies, and other irrelevancies from the prelude to your presentation.

Here are seven lucky bonuses gained by your constant application of the just-one-client concept:

1. You'll avoid unpleasant blunders
2. You'll gain ego control
3. You'll eliminate small talk
4. You'll increase selling efficiency
5. You'll increase selling time
6. You'll build mutual respect
7. You'll close sales faster

The Client and the Client's Success are Paramount

The Just-One-Client concept is a very satisfying selling nuance. It's comfortable. Having all of your thoughts, sales points, and reason-why's entirely focused on the client is a most pleasant posture for you to be in. You're startled and quickly reverse if you hear yourself slipping into "I," "me," or "my."

The secret of making JOC work for you is this:

- Rehearse every presentation to give it total JOC thrust.
- Make it habitual, an easy and natural technique.
- Forget about personal preamble. Remember that it usually causes you to talk about *your* spouse, *your* children, *your* hobby.
- Fervently avoid reference to any other business of yours. The only important business is this client's. He or she is the most important person in the world right now. If the client asks "How's business," be careful. Turn it back to his or her business. There are exceptions,

of course, where other buyers of your product are valuable endorsement, but no endorsement means as much as the values of your product for this particular client.

6. HOW TO BE TRULY FABULOUS

This is one attitude for which you do literally psyche yourself. Being fabulous is a potent antidote against being dull. A dull salesperson is an anathema to the selling profession. Your consciousness of the ever-present need to be fabulous will actually make you more so.

In a world of positive, persuasive people there is no winning place for the lackluster, bored, or uninspired. Therefore, establishing your system to make you still more fabulous is an investment you can't afford to overlook.

An Open Door to Selling Greatness

Eight steps to make you more fabulous:

1. Know it's a controllable, developable attitude.
2. Want to literally be fabulous.
3. Demand it of yourself.
4. Use the idea springboard.
5. Find appropriate devices.
6. Apply total integrity.
7. Give it total knowledge.
8. Recognize that being fabulous is unlimited in scope.

Some people are naturally more fabulous than others. Their personalities, their wit, their appearance all add up to give them a built-in edge. However, a hazard exists for the easy-come attributes. Often the effort isn't there to expand the natural qualities. If you are less naturally endowed with fabulous characteristics—like most of us—but you know you can control, expand, and build your own attitude, *you will*. And you'll usually pass the easy-comers. It's the old turtle/hare fable.

Two men come to mind. One had great natural fabulousness. The moment I first met him, I found his presence electrifying. He was in a small job, and later I learned that he was an alcoholic who had gone all the way to the gutter in the Bowery of New York. This job was his first after drying out. His reentry was sparkling, and he swooped past a horde of people to a high-level position. The last I knew of him was some publicity about him and a famous actress in Hollywood. From there back to oblivion.

The other man has it, too, but he built it. He *knows* that the quality of being fabulous can never be taken for granted. And he works at it. Hard. This man can become the President of the United States. No doubt about it. But the job doesn't pay enough. My fabulous friend is also greedy. He will be fabulously rich. However, I'm positive he'll always remain a fabulous guy.

It's Yours for the Asking

You have to know its value, and want it. You have to want it badly. That's the second step. First, you know for certain that fabulousness is yours for the asking; then, second, you need to hunger for it. Simple? Not really. There are many of your contemporaries who might label it as ostentatious. "Just make lots of calls," they say, "and be a good guy, with a smile, a joke and a handshake. I'll do all right."

They will do just that—"all right." That's not nearly good enough for achieving the winning edge in selling. It's settling for mediocrity.

The third step is demanding of yourself that you be fabulous. This is where the psyching comes in. I can clearly recall when I first demanded it of myself. I was sitting in the reception room of Dancer, Fitzgerald and Sample Advertising Agency in New York. It was a very important call for a vital piece of business. The preparatory homework had been done and rehearsed for much of the preceding night. As I sat waiting, I suddenly surprised myself by saying repeatedly under my breath, "Be fabulous. Be fabulous. Damn you, be fabulous!"

An hour or so later I practically danced out into the sunshine of Madison Avenue with the order in hand. But most of all was a realization that something new—a powerful new force—had come into my life. I had demanded of myself: *Be fabulous*. I was. It worked. And I knew that in all of my prior years I really hadn't been very exciting, interesting, or unusual. But now it was there. I could be as fabulous as I desired. All I had to do was *demand it* of myself.

The Strong Idea Creates Fabulousness

Your fourth step in becoming truly fabulous is to use the *idea* as a springboard. As we previously showed, ideas are exciting. You become more fabulous as a salesperson when you excite, stimulate, and motivate. Innovation is the trigger. It sets off a charge of responses. Response often leads to the order. We've said it before; it bears repeating: There is an idea waiting to fit any situation. Your imagination finds the idea.

Find the Dramatic Assist

There are props which fit appropriately into helping to make you a more fabulous salesperson. Appropriate devices are available to fit almost any product or service. It could be over-worked, but more often it evokes, "She's fabulous. I wonder what she'll come up with next." Finding and using interesting, attention-getting, or humorous props, is the fifth step towards making you a more fabulous salesperson. Your fabulousness is limited only by your imagination, and imagination is limitless.

We've already told you about some of our props. The giant with top hat, swirling open his cape to reveal "For the Giant Sales Gains Go Eastman." The rhinestones on a black velvet pad—"Pick out the diamond." The salesperson, putting a match to a dollar bill and stating "What a waste! Let's save some bucks for you."

Not only are these selling devices part of your being more fabulous, they're fun provoking. And thought provoking. A book, a rose, a handful of coins, a sign, a pen, a necktie—all can tie into some situation. It takes only imagination—thinking—and you add another notch to your fabulousness.

In my company being fabulous was a sales meeting subject from time to time. Bill B., whom I have introduced to you on a few occasions before, latched onto "Be fabulous" and made it part of his personal trademark. All of his letters are signed, not Yours truly, Sincerely, Cordially, or With best wishes, but Be Fabulous. Bill B. is now president of that company and earning a fine income.

The Fabulous Quality of Integrity

From the sublime to the serious. The sixth step towards your goal is making integrity a kind of holy grail. You cannot be fabulous without it. Also, it is a very comforting trait to live with. The salesperson with total integrity isn't constantly looking over his or her shoulder, concerned about being apprehended in a falseness.

One straying misstep away from total integrity utterly destroys whatever fabulousness had been attained. You saw it happen to a President of the United States, a Vice President, and several Representatives.

Having the Facts Makes You Fabulous

Don R. is a great friend and, as I write this, a key member of the Cabinet of the United States. We were discussing a truly fabulous thirty-four year old in Washington and Don said, "When they oppose him, he counters with a barrage of incontrovertable facts. His knowledge is fantastic."

Total knowledge is your seventh step to becoming even more fabulous. Of course, total is a goal, never reached, but always reached for.

It may be quite possible for you to master all of the facts about your product and your industry. There are exceptions. Who could know all the sizes, styles and prices in a Sears catalogue, for example? However, your pertinent sales data is always more readily assimilated for instant retrieval because it spells money. Having the key facts—all of the meaningful ones—in your mind makes you a more fabulous salesperson. Try to know more than anyone else about your particular field. It's well worth the effort.

The very fact that you are reading this book leads me to believe that you are already a fabulous salesperson. Seeking new concepts, new techniques, and different nuances to build your winning advantage should automatically expand your quality of fabulousness. The eighth step to make you more fabulous is your firm realization that this marvelous trait is unlimited in its scope.

Many salespersons reach a certain achievement and level off there. In some organizations this is acceptable. "There have to be Indians," it's said, "we can't all be chiefs." Don't buy it! Never accept that cliché. In every day of your sales career there's both a need and an opportunity to improve. Sell more, earn more. Settling into a satisfying rut holds no allure. That's why fear, greed, and shrewdness aren't negative attributes, they're building blocks to being more fabulous.

Observe competitors who *think* they are hot shots. Flamboyant clothing, ostentatious jewelry, the expensive car—all "me" props. It's promoting personal ego. This unfabulous characterization often includes questionable slickness, "A special deal for you only." Expedient selling.

Use this eight-step plan to double your fabulous net worth frequently. A new idea, a new selling nuance, a new system, a new sales device—but most of all a prevailing attitude to be more fabulous—and you will be!

Summary

You have the means to create those beneficial attitudes that guarantee you a strong winning edge:

   I. Make emotions such as fear, greed, and uncertainty work for you.
  II. Always hasten to correct an error—positively.
 III. Keep sickness in healthy perspective.
 IV. Master the studied negative.
  V. Build your Just-One-Client concept.
 VI. Follow the eight steps to being fabulous.

There you have a half-dozen sales banners. These attitudinal nuances will bring a bundle of new dollars to your bottom line.

7 ESTABLISH YOUR INDIVIDUAL TRADEMARK— YOUR I.T.

- Find your best assets to build on
- Put the two parts together—the invisible and the visible
- Cultivate sources to expand and preserve your I.T.

THREE FUNDAMENTAL STEPS
TO CREATE YOUR STRONGER I.T.

1. Identify, examine, and rank your personal and persuasive basic assets

2. Apply the underlying invisible foundation elements to your I.T.

3. Add numerous visible surface factors to make your I.T. more marketable

ndividualism is an essential ingredient towards the objective of building an ever-growing winning edge in selling. It is the force that makes an outstanding, productive, and high-earning salesperson. You stand out above the crowd because you have taken the time to make yourself unique. And better.

You Are the Product

The process of creating your own special individualism requires a carefully thought-out plan. Contrary to governmental edicts, we are definitely not all created equal. Each of us possesses pronounced variants of body size and shape, features, personality, speech—right down to the fingerprints. We are most unequal in the components that make each of us an unprecedented human being. And that's good.

But Equal in Opportunity

Making allowances for certain uncommon exceptions, each person holds the capacity to create a very unequal, unorthodox, and extraordinary product of himself or herself. This is an unending process, especially towards that objective of creating your highly individual trademark in selling. The opportunity to achieve personal prominence by means of having and executing your plan is totally equal and open to everyone just for the doing.

The problem is, very few people ever really sit down and ask themselves the vital questions: What am I? What are my strengths? What can I do to put together a better total personal package, a highly individualistic product? To build the kind of a trademark for me that creates a more effective salesperson?

Take Inventory and Take Action

This process of refurbishing yourself into a more highly identifiable salesperson requires first your taking inventory of all of your personal assets. Then, by applying some of our ideas and many of yours, you build a plan to work more profits out of those basic assets. We will demonstrate several nuances and unorthodoxies that will help to lead the way to your winning more income through a well-developed and well-exploited individual trademark. Let's call it your I.T. quotient.

It Can't Be Left to Chance

Most people just evolve. A specific system and a plan is missing. They grow—and many grow exceptionally well—but they would grow a strong I.T. much earlier if it were not left to chance. We're after that exceptional winning edge in selling. The more things we do right sooner, the faster we expand our income. That's the goal—money. It's the best measure of achievement. And its usefulness is paramount.

1. IDENTIFY, EXAMINE, AND RANK YOUR PERSONAL AND PERSUASIVE BASIC ASSETS

As part of the inventory-taking process, on a sheet of paper write a list of all your personal attributes. Try to be objective, neither too complimentary nor too critical. Make it a fair appraisal. Give this introspective exercise considerable thought. Possibly check with your spouse or a close friend who is willing to sincerely evaluate your measurements of yourself. This is not a plan to make you over. It is simply a method geared to maximize what you already have going for you.

A certain very good friend comes to mind. It wouldn't be difficult to draw up a rather long list. But getting to the bottom line, here's the list of his best personal attributes:

Has strong empathy.
Meets people easily.
Is an eager expansionist.
Is a ready risk-taker.
Enjoys dealing and selling.
Has high integrity.
Has good financial instincts.

How do those seven personal attributes meld into part of his individual trademark? With very little training or prior experience, he has molded these traits into becoming a successful entrepreneur in the retail business. An entrepreneur with a thriving self-made enterprise certainly has a rather good I.T. A closer inspection, study, and weighing of these assets, merged with elements that follow, would easily convert his "rather good" I.T. to a superb one. This very good friend just happens to be my son.

Achieving a recognized level of attainment is a huge part of the I.T. It's the visible tip of the iceberg. As you will see, there's much more under the surface.

Build Your Balance Sheet of Personal Differences

With your list in hand, examine each item with an eye towards those offering you the greatest growth possibility. Put an asterisk on those meriting further consideration. Rank them in order of their significance. Gradually you will see a new you emerging. That new you will have a more distinct individualism.

Here's an I.T. Worth Millions

Fred H., president of a pump manufacturing company, developed his individual trademark from salesman to executive to visionary. This story exemplifies the ultimate value of the I.T. Also, its cash value.

"We were being pursued more and more," Fred says. "It was an era of many mergers and acquisitions. I seemed to be spending half my time talking to corporate development people who were interested in our company, so we began to get serious."

He continues, "I found it extremely valuable to develop a concept and put it on paper. This involved a ten-year review of fiscal progress. Also I wrote a long-term plan for five years in the future. This included financial projections, balance sheets, and profit and loss forecasts—plus a good conceptual approach of what we were trying to do with the business.

"What are we," Fred asked himself, "a pump manufacturer? Well, specifically, precisely, yes. But much more than that. We were in the total program of water resources, water supply, water pollution control."

By expanding his I.T. from executive to visionary, Fred put his company in an attractive position to be acquired by an outstanding Fortune 500 corporation. To become more of a visionary, Fred expanded his innovative powers. That imaginative-conceptual process created strong personal I.T. values.

"It was an excellent deal from our standpoint and theirs. For both the future of our company and the individuals involved, it's been progress ever since." Fred concluded, "It seems to me all this proves is that if you package your well-considered facts into a well-organized concept, you'll be successful. Isn't that what selling is all about?"

Fred's highly profitable, well-organized concept grew from his I.T., which was founded on basic personal assets. It's almost always that way. They buy a person.

Put It All Together

Five ways to mold your personal traits:

1. Build an initial list.
2. Add to it as you study it.
3. Asterisk your leading indicators.
4. Rank your plusses in order of their significance.
5. Begin to conceive how these implement the expansion of your I.T.

Because you become what you are capable of becoming *and* what you want to be, those five simple steps point you in the right direction.

Move on From Personal Attributes to Persuasive Attributes

Next analyze your *persuasive attributes.* As an example, here's what your list might be:

- Thorough preparation
- Thoughts keyed exclusively to prospect needs
- Good use of sales questions
- Good listening

- Constant closing cues
- Strong summary of customer gains
- Friendly, but serious demeanor

Merge Into a Highly Identifiable Individual Trademark

Place your lists of personal attributes and persuasive attributes side by side. At first glance they may not seem to relate. Then gradually you will begin to envision what your individual trademark should be or should be altered into. These fundamental assessments of what you are spotlight what you can become. The objective is to maximize everything you have going for you. Through using this simple self-evaluation plan, you emphasize your strengths, both personally and persuasively, and you place yourself as a strong individual. You thereby become much more than just one of a herd of salespersons.

2. APPLY THE UNDERLYING INVISIBLE FOUNDATION ELEMENTS TO YOUR I.T.

By carefully weighing your basic personal and persuasive traits, you will gradually arrive at certain conclusions. It will become clear that more emphasis on various attributes and somewhat less on others will substantially strengthen this fundamental foundation to your growing I.T.

Forge Your I.T. Vitality

Recognizing that your fundamental assets must be coordinated to the best balance is primary. The result may be invisible to your customers. However, the resultant increased efficiency, vitality, and sales results will be readily visible to you and your associates.

One company videotapes its sales staff's presentations. On the replay they critique the performance and suggest improvements in the approach, content, and overall impression. It's an excellent exercise, permitting both salesperson and associates to observe him or her in action. The constructive criticism is very meaningful.

The Dale Carnegie Sales Course puts participants on their

feet to speak to the group, followed by analysis of the performance. From this aspect of the Dale Carnegie method, salespersons gain many improvements in style, presence, and self-confidence. There's much more to it than that, of course. I urge every salesperson who hasn't done it to take advantage of this type of training.

But the Best Comes Only From You

Knowing that most of your I.T. must emanate from your own private evaluations is essential. This doesn't negate other supplementary avenues of improvement. However, your self-help through balancing basic assets is the most direct and effective means of achieving the winning edge, not only sooner, but also on a firm foundation.

Charley A. is a superb young salesperson. His career to date is in insurance. He realizes the lifetime career values of building towards the epitome of professional salesmanship. To him being a salesperson is equal in achievement, stature, and remuneration to becoming a leading surgeon, C.E.O. of a major corporation, or proprietor of a prospering enterprise. He knows, of course, that the quality of professional salesmanship is the key to the C.E.O. office or one's own insurance business.

A continuous effort towards improved selling methods is as basic to Charley as sleeping, eating, and working. His individual trademark is one that would be ranked by most of his customers and associates as excellent. It's not good enough for him.

"Selling just a contract—words on paper, guarantees against loss—is such an intangible," he says. "Possibly more than in the selling of any other product, the individual selling elements have very strong bearing. It constantly calls for seeking new ways to improve methods to a higher level of efficiency. This then makes the time for expanded sales contact."

At first the suggestion of building a stronger individual trademark evoked skepticism. "Too general," Charley said, shrugging. Then we sat down to list his balance sheet of personal and persuasive basic assets. His interest perked when he realized that the system wasn't just theory.

Subsequently, Charley carefully analyzed his personal

and persuasive assets and found that a more efficient utilization of his natural abilities did indeed give him a much
stronger individual trademark. With this extra power working
for him, he was able to close sales faster.

"Now I get right to the prospect's benefits faster. That's
the name of the game—what's in it for the client, for how
much." Charley laughed, "Then I pause and listen intently,
answer objections, and next I offer the contract and the pen."

Charley figured that his revised method was enabling him
to get in at least one more call per day. From the sparkle in
his eye and his enthusiastic outlook, it was easy to perceive
the growing I.T.—and the growing commissions. The results
were probably not readily discernible to Charley's clients, but
anyone knowing the plan behind it could appreciate his new
I.T. and the results it was creating.

3. ADD NUMEROUS VISIBLE SURFACE FACTORS TO MAKE YOUR I.T. MORE MARKETABLE

Growing a great money-making individual trademark is impossible without the basics in place. Although the visibles are the
obvious part of a blossoming I.T., they become quickly super-
ficial and meaningless without the solid underlying efficiency
of well-balanced basics. Also, the I.T. lacks selling drama without good visibles.

Synchronizing the Two I.T. Elements

Finding that your functioning basics actually create much of
your visibles is a happy discovery. It does not obviate the need
for further specific actions. There's a long list of things that go
into the visibles. Here's a short one:

- Attitudes
- Dress
- Personality
- Systems

This list subdivides almost infinitely. Chapter 6 covered the
important subject of creating attitudes, but what wasn't said
was how many of the beneficient attitudes add to the I.T. It is

inevitable that some of our concepts and systems overlap and seem redundant. For example, as you become more fabulous, that too becomes a vital part of your individual trademark. Taking a look at specifics will demonstrate the extra I.T.-builders found in various nuances.

Build Your I.T. With Exceptional Telephone Talent

Imagine trying to function in business without that magical instrument of communications, the telephone. This sales tool affords several opportunities to expand your I.T.

1. Avoid hiding behind it.
2. Use a private line.
3. Let it ring.
4. Develop a greeting style.
5. Improve the voice.
6. Conquer the distance problem.

"Who's calling?" or "May I tell Ms. Adams who's calling?" are negatives. They create instant barriers. One envisions Ms. Adams hiding behind the protective screen of her secretary. Another negative is "Ms. Adams is in a meeting." The impression often conveyed is one of exaggerated importance.

It literally amazed me this morning to get a "Who's calling" from the office of an exceptional salesperson. It reminded me that I could help avoid the negative by announcing, "This is Bob Eastman, may I please speak to Mr. Carson?"

Recognizing and correcting these misuses of the telephone adds to your visible I.T. Convert negatives to positives. The best way is answering your phone in person: "Hello! Jane Adams here." If circumstances require someone else to answer your telephone, insist that they give it a very cheerful, "Hello! Jane Adams's office." The rest is just good routine—but take steps to be sure it is *good*.

It seems that many of my acquaintances and associates are named Bill. Well, this particular Bill is the chairman of one of the Fortune 500 companies. He was formerly president of one of the principal divisions of the company. It registered

a deep impression on me that almost always when I tele-
phoned him, he immediately answered the call in person. If
he wasn't there, his secretary sounded truly sorry when she
said, "Oh, Mr. L. will be sorry to have missed you." This positive approach didn't come about by happenstance.

A *private line,* answered only by you, has advantages.
Giving this number to clients can be a small complimentary
touch. They know that if their ring isn't answered, you're out
selling. To leave a message, they call the switchboard or your
secretary. Your direct availability via the private line enables
the essential telephone use to add an extra plus to your I.T.

Letting it ring is an important concept. The customer who
is there in your place of business is always a priority over
someone telephoning in. It's astonishing how often this good
business fundamental is violated. Your I.T. expands when you
ignore the ring and focus your entire attention on the customer
who has taken the time and trouble to come and see you. If
the ringing is persistent and annoying to your discussion, a
fast, friendly "Call you back" disposes of it.

A greeting style can be a positive visible facet of I.T. The
cliché dialogue:

> "Hello! Jane Adams here."
> "Hello, Jane."
> "Hi Frank, how are you?"
> "Fine thanks, how are you?"

Neither is really requesting a summary of health symptoms,
but that is sometimes the result of such a dialogue.

The better I.T. approach:

> "Hello! Jane Adams here."
> "Hello, Jane."
> "Why, Frank, you old scoundrel, good to hear from you."
> "How are you, Jane?"
> "Wild and wooly, just waiting for you!"

The voice at the switchboard is especially meaningful, as it
affects the company trademark—and indirectly yours, too. One
company, a competitor, has the best operator. Her voice, diction, and style really give that company a touch of class. We

faced a constant frustration trying to get close to that competitive plus.

Another company, a very large one, seems to cultivate harsh, abrupt, cold voices at their switchboard. You wonder why it isn't corrected. Everyone in a management capacity shares the blame.

The distance problem for any salesperson doing business with remote customers is ever-present. It requires awareness of it and positive steps to overcome it. When someone repeatedly telephones you from hundreds of miles away, and the phone just rings and rings, an inevitable picture of goofing off or lack of interest arises in the mind of that caller. If it happens to you, cover it fast with an appropriate apology: "Joe, I'm terribly sorry to have missed you."

Laugh and Your Customer Laughs With You

Ed L. has a fine, sincere, ringing laugh. He wasn't born with it. I suspect it developed out of a genuine affection for people, enthusiasm generated from his highly successful selling results and the fact that his laugh evokes laughter. A good laugh is a sales tool and adds greatly to your I.T. You can cultivate a laugh best by letting it spring from excitement—it will bubble forth with sincerity.

C. Northcote Parkinson, promulgator of Parkinson's First Law, "Work expands to fill the time available," told a young man about a sixth law: "Don't take yourself too seriously." You bet that he guffawed as he offered that advice. Your good laugh comes from developing a sense of humor and "Not taking yourself too seriously." Humor underlies every situation.

Cultivate I.T. Gestures

Debate with Fred H. and he raises his eyebrows, smiles, and pulls on an earlobe, "Yes, but . . ." It's his gentle way of countering. We have discussed gestures before and undoubtedly will again. This facet of expression is such an integral part of winning selling that it bears repetition and reevaluation as it relates to various subjects. Your individual trademark calls for certain individual gestures. These movements of the hands, body, face, eyes are most assuredly a developed attribute.

Nobody is born with a ready-made set of interesting gestures. Actors create gestures to fit the script. As a salesperson in action, you are on stage. Your specialized gestures become an interesting part of your entire presentation. A good set of gestures is a strong visible part of your I.T.

John F., former sales executive with one of America's finest manufacturing companies, told me, "You have to think outside yourself." As I digested that interesting thought, John went on, "Then your gestures, your entire approach, fits the prospect. You don't have to have a pat, predictable act."

Find the Right Gestures and Rehearse Them

You've got to have gestures and they have to fit you. Many people simply imitate normal gestures. Others let it just kind of come naturally. Very little is normal or natural to the attaining of the winning edge. Like winning at anything, it requires that exceptional extra effort.

Through observation you can make a long list of gestures. Watch tv and movies with a pad and pencil. As you jot down certain gestures, think how they could relate to selling situations. Next, determine which ones appeal to you and how you may alter them to work some of them into your exclusive I.T.

Rehearsing your acquired gestures in front of a mirror until they become a comfortable part of you is the only way I know of to improve this aspect of your selling technique. Even if your present set of selling gestures seem quite satisfactory, analyze them to determine if yours are truly individualistic. Perhaps you may wish to gradually add some different gestures to both enhance your I.T. and put extra dramatic impact into your singular approach.

Expand your winning I.T. with better gestures to:

1. Demonstrate
2. Dramatize
3. Convince
4. Make your ideas flow
5. Respond
6. Use your face better
7. Use your body better

8. Use your hands better

Don W., my car dealer friend, uses gestures that are all demonstrative of the product. Patting, smoothing, pointing, measuring—his every movement fits a quality of the automobile. And the vehicle grows in value before your eyes. His face smiles, frowns, eyebrows go up, lips purse. His head nods, inclines, moves side to side. His body shrugs, leans forward, leans backwards. All of Don's movements synchronize into a studied, practiced, and effective demonstration of the merits of his product.

Every salesperson will find ready rewards from analyzing, improving, and rehearsing his or her package of gestures. With better coordinated use of the face, the hands, the body, your concepts will flow more readily.

Listening improves, too. My friend Jack B., during many years in the securities business, has developed a marvelous set of listening/responding gestures. His head nods, smile broadens, restrained palms-up affirms gains, hands move apart slightly to respond to client's reference to size or amount. It's all a smooth listening response.

Clichés Are Anti-I.T.

Wiping out clichés is absolutely essential to building your individual trademark. Some salespersons seem to revel in a flow of trite sayings: "Oh, well, better late than never." "A stitch in time, you know." "Hah, hah, better safe than sorry." They've studiously found an old saying to fit almost any situation. The endless list of worn-out words probably was inherited from parents. Those tired phrases deserve only the junkyard. Good, strong slogans sparingly applied are another thing.

Originality of expression adds to the difference between you and others. Your differences of *thought*, *action*, and *speech* create your growing individual trademark.

Reappraise the Obvious Visibles of the I.T.

There are certain other I.T.-building visibles so apparent that their inclusion here would seem unnecessary. But sometimes the most obvious aspects do require at least a passing over. Yesterday I was discussing the elements of this chapter with a couple of friends. Both are successful sales executives. One said, "How do you dress if you're calling on farmers?" Suffice it to say, appropriate dress is a matter of good taste and good judgment. However, taste and judgment may vary to an extreme with individuals. It does require some appraisal to fit you better to your market. Personally, I endorse some facet of attire that adds to your I.T. Whatever it is, it should be pleasing, unostentatious, and unprovoking of discussion. Your special, personal-dress touch simply says quietly it is you. One of my personal preferences is a blue shirt with a white tie.

Avoid Offensive Negatives

One of our best salespeople had a breath problem. Another had a bad case of dandruff. We had the one with the bad dandruff tell the other one about his bad breath and vice versa. No offense; problems corrected.

When I was a child, one of my front teeth was broken. In business I knew that my smile left something to be desired. It wasn't until about age forty that a business associate blurted out, "Why in the hell don't you get your front teeth fixed?" I did and, man, how I smiled thereafter!

Summary

Following these I.T.-building concepts adds vastly to your competence, confidence, and compensation:

I. Identify, examine, and rank your personal and persuasive basic assets.
II. Apply the underlying invisible foundation elements to your I.T.
III. Add numerous visible surface factors to make your I.T. more marketable.

Applying these three guidelines will give you extra power. There's a flow of strong benefits from creating your distinctive individual trademark. You gain confidence, respect, and a subtle mystique. Most of all, your more-potent personal sales package gains a winning edge that is spelled $ $ $!

8 MASTER THE POWER OF POSITIVENESS

- Discover a new income-building quality
- Learn simple techniques that bring you extra sales power
- Attain a higher level of overall performance potency

YOUR FIVE STEPS TO A SUPERB UNIQUE SELLING POWER

1. Recognize the secret power of a new kind of positiveness

2. Apply this power effectively

3. Learn the positive gestures; avoid the negative

4. Develop your positive give-to-get system

5. Find new power in positive respect

1. RECOGNIZE THE SECRET POWER
OF A NEW KIND OF POSITIVENESS

This power is a total *can-do* dedication. Highly contagious, it is supported by both facts and action, working miracles in business, science, government, and sales. It is an overwhelming force that refuses any semblance of denial.

The winning edge in selling is replete with this indomitable power of positiveness. We will describe, in the pages of this chapter, the nuances, concepts, and systems to build more of this great force into your selling. We will demonstrate how you amplify this compulsion into ever-growing sales and income.

There is a distinct and significant difference between the power of positiveness (P.O.P.) and *The Power of Positive Thinking* made famous by Norman Vincent Peale. Although both are closely related, an oversimplification is that one is thought and the other (P.O.P.) is action. P.O.P. is an overt force expended by you to create positive response, convertible into sales. P.O.P. is a successful selling technique.

Ring Your Personal Cash Register With New P.O.P.

Undoubtedly you, as a professional salesperson, already possess a good share of this P.O.P. Otherwise you'd never ring a doorbell or walk in on a cold prospect. Our goal is to lead the way for you to literally *own* this potent sales weapon. All of it.

Six ways you gain total P.O.P.:

1. By assuming that all prospects are inundated with uncertainties.
2. By knowing that your P.O.P. attitude is contagious.
3. By discarding all weak, uncertain expressions.
4. By replacing weak uncertain qualifiers with strong positive ones.
5. By rehearsing your presentations to insure total P.O.P.

6. By using this new kind of P.O.P. to stage quicker closings.

Because of the perennial existence of uncertainties, salesmanship is always in high demand. A vital part of our daily sales task is converting uncertainties into certainties. It's a pleasant process because people are inevitably happier on the solid ground of the known rather than the unknown. The secret power of positiveness flourishes as a winning sales tool mainly because customers desire this kind of strong conviction. It allays their doubts.

Miles D., the Don Quixote With Great P.O.P.

As president of an industry association, Miles D. fought the windmills with total P.O.P. Most people today recognize and accept radio as a necessity of life. It fulfills a communication need in kitchens, cars, bedrooms, and bathrooms that no other medium penetrates as effectively. It wasn't always understood this way.

When Miles began jousting with the windmills, radio was in low repute. As Art C., member of Miles's board, astutely put it, "Nobody understands radio except the people." Newspapers were deeply entrenched as the sole medium of the vast retail establishment. TV had become the exclusive realm of the advertising agency business. Radio was obsolete.

With stubborn consistency, Miles and his associates tackled the giants head-on. One early gimmick was to tape the pages of a newspaper together, then roll it across a room with the challenge, "Okay, find your ad." But that was negative and was soon replaced with the P.O.P. of facts, facts, facts. And research.

Miles put the cold competitive facts on the line. As newspaper rates increased, circulation and readership decreased. At the same time, radio advertising costs remained lower proportionately to circulation-listening gains. As retailer doubts grew, the more vigorously did Miles and his cohorts apply the power of positiveness to convert doubters into believers.

Assailing the Sanctimonious Sanctuary of TV

At one point, Miles faced a situation in which a word against tv was profane. But research continuously confirmed that throughout the U.S., total weekly radio listening actually exceeded total tv viewing. That couldn't be kept under wraps even with the tv diehards. Call after call, presentation after presentation, and untold hours of preparation fueled a great positive effort. Miles and his team, with the full thrust of P.O.P., dramatically converted the advertising experts to a new "discovery" of radio. It became *their* idea. Radio was back in fashion.

Miles's Ultimate Bootstrap Method

In well-produced P.O.P. style, radio commercials proliferated on radio stations in every city and town in the U.S. Businesspeople listened to the radio and heard the positive facts of radio compared to newspapers and to tv.

The bottom line: Thanks to this dedicated application of P.O.P., radio today is a thriving medium with revenues soaring to new highs every year. Uncertainties were dissolved effectively with the positive power of the Miles D. approach.

The contagiousness of the power of positiveness is epidemic. It's the Pied Piper that rallies timid doubters to a cause. That cause is buying your product and expanding your income. Recognizing this contagion of P.O.P. enables you to use it lavishly, effectively, and profitably. Let me mention here that there may appear to be a contradiction between the power of positiveness and appropriate humility. However, as you will fully appreciate as this chapter progresses, there is no conflict between humility and P.O.P.

Use P.O.P. to Break a Money Logjam

Jimmy R. operated some of the best U.S. broadcasting stations. The early morning drive-time personality on one of his stations commanded top dollar in his market. It was totally sold out. What do you do when you're sold out and strong demand persists? Raise the rates! Jimmy balked. "My local sales reps just won't hold still for such an increase." I had suggested quite a hike in the price. My boss also tried to dissuade me from pressuring the matter. However, without the substantial increase to open up the SRO condition, our volume—and commissions—were dormant.

Answer: Turn on the full power of positiveness. I phoned Jimmy. "Do you mind if I meet with your local sales staff to discuss this matter?" He was skeptical, but said they'd be happy to see me anyway.

They Caught It and Bought It

The contagion of the power of positiveness was a strong basis for my strategy to sell the price increase. They were a hot local sales team, genuine enthusiasts, not a phony old pro in the group. After a round of handshakes in Jimmy's conference room and a few pertinent shoot-me-down quips, I launched my P.O.P. pitch right at their pocketbooks.

"Fellows, it's all sold out. You've no more to sell at any price," I pointed out. "Why not have none for sale at a one-third higher price?" They laughed and I felt them catching the power. "The only way you're going to make more money from this program is for it to open up a little. When it does, the 33⅓ percent increase will be a cinch."

The objections were minimal. Their local sales had stagnated, too. A few spots available in the highly desirable morning drive time would also tie in sales of other time periods. I pointed that out, and soon the heads were nodding unanimous agreement.

A $100,000 Sale

That was what the increase was worth to our national volume, not to mention local volume gains. Jimmy was surprised at the ease of the sale. Previously his local staff was adamantly opposed to the price increase. They had only related it to *my* commission gain, not to their own incomes. The direct positive approach to *their* income put a very different light on the matter.

Jimmy's salespeople, being bright, aggressive, and always hungry, were readily infected with P.O.P. Salespeople generally are more responsive to an injection of this power. But, acting on the theory that everyone in business is a salesperson, to a certain degree, you may be sure that customers can catch the bug of P.O.P. too. Whenever your well-founded positive approach dissolves some of those ever-present uncertainties of a customer he or she is beginning to catch it. And you're in the process of catching another sale.

Use the Science of Semantics

You can be sure that your application of semantics is a scientifically certain way of making more sales with P.O.P. All of those formerly identified bad clichés are negatives. "To tell the truth," "Frankly," "Now to be perfectly truthful," "Honestly," and such, are terrible words from the mouths of salespeople. Recently we've been seeing a lot of a white-maned old-pro politician on tv. Every time he growls out, "Now to be perfectly truthful . . ." thousands of viewers must be sharing the thought: What was he saying earlier that was untruthful?

Your further semantic advancement, beyond those most obvious ones above, is in eradicating all "maybes," "perhapses," "possiblys," "incidentallys"—all those tentative utterances. They only add to customer uncertainty because you are saying words that imply that you aren't totally secure either.

P.O.P. Is Total Confidence, Total Assurance

It is a strange phenomenon to note the prevalence of weak semantics. If you are unaware of the extent of this sales weakness, listen for it. It's there. Some use it mistakenly attempting to add some warmth and humility to their words. Others feel obliged to cushion a strong positive statement with a tentative utterance.

The confidence and assurance that flows from the P.O.P. concept is largely fueled by strong positive semantics. It's all upbeat. "Maybes" dissolve into "absolutelys." It's not a case of overstatement, and doesn't come across that way when properly executed. It is a successful technique, one diametrically different from the studied negative. It flows from an enthusiastic, powerfully positive method of presentation.

Of course, you use the P.O.P. technique frequently and with success. It's a natural good-selling inclination. However, through better recognition of this power, and the proper language that goes with it, you will make it a far stronger sales weapon. You will use P.O.P. more overtly and with more regularity, to your advantage.

Let me hasten to point out that there is nothing negative about the studied negative (chapter 6). It is a *positive* technique to be applied to certain situations and certain prospects to trap them into singing your song. It's a good positive sales trap.

Rehearsing Ensures More P.O.P.

Selling, like acting, requires rehearsal. We can't be casual about a pending sale. Your words, spoken and written, need to be right. Please don't ever permit yourself to be deluded into thinking that your years of selling put you above and beyond the need for rehearsal.

There's too much tentative, weak and uncertain selling around. All you need do is listen to some of it to know that hardly anyone is giving adequate thought and rehearsal to the power of positiveness.

The other day I tested it. Harvey C. has been selling men's clothing for over twenty years. I walked in on him exclaiming, "Harvey, what have you got that will improve my personality?" This was asking for a strong positive pitch.

Harvey smiled and drawled, "Well, maybe you'd like something. . ." He led me to the racks of sport jackets. "Something . . . perhaps . . . a blue blazer. Uh, you like blue? How about this green cashmere? On sale. Or . . ."

That's a misguided, but very familiar, attempt at soft sell or low pressure. A better label is *no* sale and *no* pressure.

The Big Secret Key to Unlocking Your Full P.O.P.

Avoid the temptation to seem very sincere and very accommodating by offering a wide choice. That's the key. With P.O.P. and thoughtful rehearsal, you've made the decision of what the customer should purchase. Your thoughtfully arrived at judgment to fit your product to the customer's needs puts you right on target to the close. Who should know best about your product, you or the customer?

The impulse to offer choices drains your P.O.P. Chocolate, vanilla, or Golden Nugget? Blue, red, or green? If Harvey C. had only paused a moment to scan me for color, size, and style, instead of vacillating and confusing with choices, he'd have said, "Bob, your timing is most propitious." (Always open with a *"you"* remark, never the "I've got just what . . . .") "It's new" (that appealing word "new"), "a silver-blue cashmere . . . look great on you!" I'm a sucker for a strong, forthright, smart pitch. We all are. That's why the power of positiveness is such a potent selling tool. It's fun and easy to cultivate.

You Guarantee Faster Closing of Sales With P.O.P.

It's so logical and so absolutely simple. Your time is a prime asset. Your confident, assuring, on-target presentation of the best buy will score sales for you faster and more frequently. Sure, there is often the need to adjust, adapt, or come up with an alternative. But you will win more often by using a rifle than a shotgun loaded with choices. Manufacturers create choices, astute salespersons create decisions.

2. HOW YOU APPLY THIS POWER EFFECTIVELY

You already own an abundance of P.O.P. Your pursuit of the winning edge is proof enough. Like almost everything in winning selling, the successful techniques are yeasty—very expanding. And, like yeast, your income expands rapidly with the application of these techniques. None are theory. All have been tested over many years in both sales training and personal selling. Many well-to-do salespersons have emerged with the assistance of concepts such as the Power of Positiveness.

Awareness Is Basic

You must believe in it. The old pro, tossing his envelope on the customer's desk with, "Pick out what you want and let me know," probably never heard of or thought about the power of positiveness. Yet, you can be sure, many people consider "Old Pro" a rather good salesperson—easy to get along with, friendly, doesn't offend. But he doesn't sell. Some orders come across his desk, enough to make his unperceptive boss think that Old Pro is a "Good Joe."

Just being constantly aware of the significance of P.O.P. gives you an advantage. If you make yourself aware of it, you'll be using it. It works. Your sales will jump. Next thing you know, P.O.P. is a firm habit.

Nurture It

Fertilizing your P.O.P. is essential to ensure its growth. Human nature, being what it is, works against the winning edge. It's not just prevalent laziness, but also, a tendency to let up on strong selling. You've launched into a couple of fine, positive, on-target presentations with customer A. You closed two good sales. Now comes the temptation to make a low-pressure, service, no-pitch call. Why? It just feels right.

With an amazing technique like P.O.P. that always works, nurture it. Never turn it off. "That Bill Smith! . . . always selling." Music to the ears of a sales manager or a spouse who appreciates ascending commission checks.

Quell Uncertainties

Soft-sell, offering choices, and just-stopped-in-to-say-hello brand of nonselling, not only doesn't earn money, it doesn't help the customer either. It fails to alleviate any uncertainties or solve any problems. A soothing interval call is a waste. Keep selling. With P.O.P.

Some Variations on the Theme

Routine selling can get boring to both the customer and the salesperson. Consistent application of P.O.P. need never suffer from such a sickness. Being fabulous is your assurance of never being dull. But the manner in which you make yourself fabulous is in your entry and in your presentation, which is always somewhat difficult. There are unlimited variations in approach, sequencing, and props to keep each call on a customer interesting for both of you.

An enthusiastic entry needn't always be loud. Remember your six-way voice mechanism—loud, soft, high, low, slow, fast. Voicing is part of the P.O.P. technique. On many occasions a whisper may be more effective than a shout.

Imagination Keeps P.O.P. Working

In your preparation you decide, from facts and judgment, what you are going to present. You try to eliminate all choices. Next you turn your imagination loose. You review your last call on this customer, and seek ideas to give the upcoming call a different approach, a totally new feel. You're the same actor, with the same audience, but in a new role.

Let's say, for instance, on the last call you did a stand-up, over-the-desk, full-throttle pitch. The next time, sit close, talk soft, but sell with the same positiveness. Third time, prop it by tossing three twenty-five-cent pieces on the desk, with a smile. When the client says, "What's this?" you reply, "Your savings on each of our units," and go on from there towards a close.

By using your imagination to always keep it different, you eradicate the temptation to insert an occasional soft-sell, no-sale call. The customer will be glad to see you, will be wondering what you're going to come up with next, and will buy.

Your four easy keys to apply P.O.P. effectively:

1. Be constantly aware of the need for P.O.P.
2. Keep it nurtured.
3. Use variations on your methods.
4. Turn on imagination to ensure some significant difference in each call.

3. LEARN THE POSITIVE GESTURES, AVOID THE NEGATIVE

Here we go again on that perennial subject of gestures. It fits every aspect of selling and is absolutely vital to your power of positiveness and building a big winning edge in your selling. A wooden Indian might have identified cigar stores at one time, but it never sold any cigars.

My friend, Roger M., made a small fortune selling real estate. Everybody who bought a house, it seemed at one point in time, bought it through Roger. He seemed to sell with a minimum of effort. As I bought my house through Roger, and some years later sold it through him, too (as many people did), I analyzed his amazing, successful technique.

Roger had a repertoire of compelling positive gestures. His broad smile would shift quickly to a serious demeanor toward serving the customer. His head moved constantly, nodding on advantages, wagging to erase problems. When a buyer pointed out a serious defect, Roger frowned, waved the back of his hand, and said, "Deduct it from the price." Then he turned on his charming smile and nodded, "I'll find out what it costs." Problem dismissed.

Over the span of a decade, I had occasion to watch Roger in action with numerous prospects. Never did I observe a negative gesture. I can't recall ever seeing him stand with his arms folded across his chest. Nor did I ever observe Roger jabbing a pointing finger at a prospect.

Positive selling gestures may not be readily noticed. They are simply part of a total effective presentation. Positive gestures are often subtle movements, gentle movements, as contrasted to wild-eyed, flailing arms. At times the raising of an eyebrow is more expressive than an arm sweep. And there are conditions where a pounding fist, or a stomping foot may be appropriate and positive. Circumstances and judgment dictate.

Also, one must find those gestures that fit best. Since gestures do become a part of personality, they are highly individualistic nuances.

Generate Gestures to Support Your Power of Positiveness

You weren't born with gestures. They grew out of a need to express yourself and achieve your desires. Because gestures are a part of personality, it is normal to accept them as they are. "I am what I am." Such an outlook misses the point that gestures are completely malleable. You can create and apply the best gestures to fit each situation. Hands, eyes, head, mouth, body, offer an infinite array of gestures. Study them. Watch others and you will see a certain triteness in the reper- toire of gestures being applied by many salespersons. A wide smile and moving arms is the gesture stock-in-trade. Different, more positive, and more appropriate means of utilizing your selling motions and expressions will add greatly to your P.O.P. and winning edge.

4. YOUR POSITIVE GIVE-TO-GET SYSTEM

The golden rule of winning selling is found in a perpetual giving method. This is a practical selling basic. Any sanctimonious overtones are not intended. It is a well-proven fundamental technique that you give to get. We said it before in Chapter 3; however, it is not only deserving of repetition, but also holds a special niche in the power of positiveness.

The Giving System Blends Into the P.O.P.

True selling is loaded with giving: Values, ideas, efficiencies, satisfactions, profits, growth, competitive advantages. You control others with a lavish offering of valuable gifts. Never is there even an implication of getting, such as a commission, winning a sales contest, seeking sympathy, or needing the business. The total give approach fits beautifully with P.O.P. Your overt positive force is subtly softened with the giving system of winning selling.

Humility Comes Automatically With the Give and the P.O.P.

An amazing technique that always works is in your finding how the power of positiveness, the giving system, and the attitude of humility are all present as a unified presentation. You don't even think about humility. Giving suffices and is adequate humility in itself. As you, a professional salesperson, recognize, this is not a complex system. Identifying it clearly, thinking about it, and rehearsing it into your daily selling builds an ever-increasing facility with this vitally strong approach. I emphasize and urge that you look upon this selling as one that is limitless in expanding your success.

How Greed Fits in

There's no contradiction between the positive giving-to-get system and greed (chapter 6). As a matter of fact, they are most compatible. As an old friend and client used to say, "You're the *gotta* boys: Gotta sell, gotta win." Greed is gotta: Gotta get that order! All of it! Giving is the essential key to gotta. Greed fails without giving. Recently this greed concept has been expressed to several highly successful businesspeople. Reaction: "Of course, what else is new?"

Allan B. is a very successful Cadillac dealer in Michigan. To many people it's a thrill to anticipate owning a Cadillac. I was no exception, although the expenditure gave pause. My reluctance to pay the price for this new luxury evaporated considerably when Allan seated me in his attractive office and, with a big smile, announced, "Your first Cadillac is free." He reached into his desk and slowly retrieved a blue velvet jewel box. Eyes glistening, he slowly extended the box toward me. "Open it up," he invited. I did and found a stunning tie clasp with a miniature Cadillac on it. It was obviously a quality piece of costume jewelry.

As my eyes widened, I'm sure, in appreciation of the most unusual and beautiful tie clasp, Allan said softly, "It's yours. Your first Cadillac." He laughed and added, "Now to the real thing!"

From one jewel to another, Allan led me around that Cadillac showroom with a full positive-giving presentation. Every feature of that gleaming automobile was a gift to me of luxury, convenience, comfort, safety, beauty. The price *almost* became inconsequential.

The Gift Opener

Launching a sale with a small gift is a proven good selling tactic. Door-openers of a free brush or a sample or a book with, "Good morning. Please accept this gift just for you," is still, and always will be, a means of establishing prospect interest. My son Bobby was selling slippers door-to-door. As the woman opened the door, he said, "Hello" and laughingly offered her a slipper saying, "If you can pull this slipper apart,

I'll give you a pair free." It worked. It got the merchandise into her hands and gave the promise of a possible gift.

Nobody gets angry over a gift. When I was calling on advertising agency time-buyers, occasionally I would go in to the call with a box in my hand—obviously a tie box—and proffer it with, "Jack, this elegant cravat was made for your personality."

Tangible Gifts Have Their Place

Wilbur L. became rich from the coal business in Providence, Rhode Island. Then he bought a radio station and found it to be more exciting than selling coal. Wilbur had pocketsful of little gifts. They were gadget gifts and fun. "You hear pearls of wisdom from commercials on WXXX." "Golden values are yours with our advertising." "The silver-toned voices of our announcers are . . . ." He offered fitting gifts with a pitch that was more humorous than convincing. But it got attention, and he was remembered. Yes, it made many sales, too.

The Ultimate, Positive Giving-to-Get Presentation

My company had lost a client in one major market and still represented him in four others. Failure to retrieve the lost radio station would jeopardize the other four and create a very serious loss of commissions. To stage an all-out effort, we invited six couples, husbands and wives, to a weekened meeting at my country club in the New York area. The logistics and planning were complex.

Our guests flew into New York City on a Friday afternoon. One of our people met each flight. All planes from various cities arrived precisely on time! Each couple was driven to their accommodations at or near the country club. In each room we gave a beautiful floral arrangement and the favorite liquor of the specific couple. A large comfortable rental car was given to each couple.

On Saturday and Sunday mornings we gave two strong, pertinent sales meetings. All of our key people gave exciting P.O.P. presentations. By careful prearrangement, the club management served absolutely rave food. After lunch the men played golf and our wives *gave* generously of their time and attention to the wives of our guests. Good luck—or providence, if you prefer—gave us three days of cool, clear weather, a rarity for New York in July.

During the morning meetings our people *gave* an abundance of ideas, sales concepts, facts, results, research. Each person was superb. There wasn't a single hitch, rough spot, or any occasion for even a momentary embarrassment.

After golf on Sunday, during the closing festivities, we *gave* trophies to our guests. Everyone, husband and wife, received something, either complimentary or humorous.

The Ultimate P.O.P. Conclusion

On Wednesday morning I received a jubilant phone call from the manager of our lost station. He gave us back the contract for his station. Subsequently in my company there was never any question or doubt about the great value of the positive giving-to-get system. On that July weekend at the Waccabuc Country Club it had been profusely demonstrated.

Ten ways to guarantee your sales success through the positive power of giving:

1. Achieve a total giving attitude
2. Find giving opportunities in every situation
3. Give ideas
4. Give data
5. Give extra benefits
6. Give of yourself, such as after-hours customer assistance
7. Give solutions to problems
8. Give pertinent, unostentatious gifts
9. Give values
10. Give your all-out power of positiveness presentation, which allays customer uncertainties and leads to an early close

5. FIND NEW POWER IN POSITIVE RESPECT

Converting others to your point of view is the goal of all applications of the power of positiveness. The fact that it works and closes sales faster is its ultimate endorsement. People want, even yearn for, positive leadership. You lead prospects to accept your reasoning and your product.

This great quality of P.O.P. is not found in being adamant or arrogant. To the contrary, it is the elimination of all timidity in your presentation, the exuding of confidence, that instills confidence. Developing and owning this power puts in your hands the great secret key to winning selling.

You Are the Product

Remember what was said in Chapter 1 about the qualities of you that make up the product. Please—right now—take a moment to review those ten basic factors in Chapter 1 to cultivate your personal banner. The tenth factor is your confidence.

The major stumbling block to gaining your full utilization of the power of positiveness is found in imperfections. Rarely is anything perfect. Have you ever known a truly perfect house? A perfect car? A perfect person? Rarely does a product fit a prospect perfectly. It we permit those imperfections to become serious problems in our minds, it is extremely unlikely that we can summon our P.O.P. into the presentation.

Give the Flaws the Back of Your Hand

As my friend, Roger M., brushed off the blemishes of a house he was selling, give the brush-off to your product's short-comings. Don't permit the imperfections to subtract from your power of positiveness.

Admittedly, sometimes there is no way to fit your product to a prospect's needs. Forget it. Wheelspins are something you can do without.

Take the worst case, with a really shabby product. That salesperson can't sell it without shabby, one-shot methods. A salesperson with any worthwhile achievement objectives will find another product to sell, one they can sell with full P.O.P. Winning salespeople are always in very high demand.

The Fire and the Fury

Misguided sales direction sometimes operates on a brand of hellfire and brimstone. "Give him hell!" "Break down the door!" "Tell him off!" "Don't accept a no!" These exhortations are intended to fire up a sleepy sales staff. The better way is with P.O.P., and giving confidence, and giving exciting new ideas to sell with.

Sell It With Love and Kindness

"Replace the love of power with the power of love." That's a quote from *The Comedy of Love* by Dr. Herbert True (produced and distributed by SMI & Co., Waco, Texas). We all seek power—power to achieve our sales goals and build our winning edge in selling, power to convert others to our point of view. But it's really not raw power that we are after. Genghis Khan, Hitler, and Mussolini exemplify the ruler with unbridled power.

The power of love is the power of giving. It is also inherent in the entire concept of the incredible power of positiveness. The confidence you exude relieves uncertainties and leads to a commitment that your prospect is happy with. There's nothing incongruous between love and a strong, fast closing. Not in my book!

Power Feeds on Power

Like the exercised muscle, which gains in strength, the more you use well-focused, intelligently applied, and giving-to-get power, the more of it you will possess. Conversely, weakness fosters more weakness. We sympathize with the weak, the sick, and the inept, but we respect the smart, the strong, and the powerful.

As you apply and build the power of positiveness in your selling, another power grows to your benefit. It's a new power found in a positive respect which flows to you. This is important. You are the product. Finding new power in positive respect goes full cycle for you from P.O.P., giving selling, respect, more P.O.P. It all builds to expand your winning edge in selling.

Summary

Your ten keys to mastering the power of positiveness:

   I. Recognize P.O.P. as a proven selling technique.
  II. Use P.O.P. to alleviate customer uncertainties.
 III. Find that P.O.P. is highly contagious.
  IV. Build your positive semantics.
   V. Rehearse presentations for maximum P.O.P.
  VI. Avoid uncertainty—make the choice in advance.
 VII. Keep your P.O.P. nurtured and growing.
VIII Expand your P.O.P. gestures.
  IX. Blend giving selling with P.O.P.
   X. Earn a new power of respect from applying P.O.P.

9 CREATIVE CLOSING TECHNIQUES THAT TIP THE BALANCE

- Discover new approaches to closing
- Reevaluate your closing methods
- Win more sales with stronger, faster closings

FOUR WAYS TO BUILD INCREASED CLOSING ABILITY

1. Apply several new approaches to the basic old problem of all selling—the close

2. Use the opening close always

3. Find your own "silver pen" closing

4. Develop the creative closing that wins more sales for you

n this chapter we are focusing on several successful techniques to enable you to close more sales and close them faster. First, we'll reexamine the elements of closing to reevaluate the relative merits of each. Second, we'll look at sequencing of elements to speed the closing process. Third, we will offer our unusual tested ideas to enable us to register more sales through a new creative closing system.

The Mystique of Closing is Bunk

So much has been said and written about closing that it has acquired a quality of mystique. "Fred is a great closer" is expressed with a reverence that implies that Fred possesses certain rare qualities that enable him to close better than almost anyone else. It is easy to begin to believe that Fred knows something the rest of us ordinary people have yet to discover.

Most of the Freds you have observed expend an undue amount of their closing vernacular in their own office. Every sale, including the transom ones, receives a great trumpeting, by Fred of course, about his masterful closing technique. Strange as it may seem, sales executives (many with shiny pants seats) dote on Fred, enjoying every word of his superbclosing, "and then I said. . . ." recitations.

The Close Is Simple

Selling experts go to great lengths in perpetuating the complexity of the close. One well-known sales course, on the subject of closing, says: "Did you ask for the order?" Well, you'll agree, that's simple enough. But it's basic, easy to do and, as we will demonstrate in various instances, fits into an unfailing positive system. Closing is nothing more than converting others to your point of view. Admittedly there are some maladroit salespersons who do manage to create a debate where none is necessary. Others, as we have pointed out previously, talk "me" and "I" instead of "you." Closing is definitely a mystique to them.

1. NEW APPROACHES TO AN OLD PROBLEM

The close, making the sale, is what it's all about. A thousand different things may assist or detract from achieving the desired result. We're going to skip certain essentials already stated and restated. But a couple of fundamentals need extra mention here:

> Be Fabulous
>
> The Y-O-U Opener
>
> The Dramatic Prop

In relating being fabulous to the subject of closing, you'll want to quickly review the last part of chapter 6 "How to Be Truly Fabulous." You are the product. The manner in which you set the stage has a strong bearing on getting to your close.

That Magic Selling Word Y-O-U

The *you* opener is a vital facet of being fabulous. Your entrance to the customer's office and your first words are vital. It's difficult for many salespersons to arrive at the firm conviction that some sort of an opening soft-shoe act is *not* necessary. To help put that misunderstanding to rest once and for all, consider that the best soft-shoe act is Y-O-U. No utterance you can contrive is more meaningful than "you." Also, consider the essential fact that nothing is more exciting, more interesting, nor more essential to the moment at hand than your product and making the sale.

Advance thought regarding your Y-O-U opening line is a key part of necessary preparation. You come on as being bright, enthusiastic, happy, and as you shake hands you state with your full power of positiveness: "Mr. Williams, you're going to earn your company about $50,000 this morning," or "Good morning, Jack. You'll really be pleased with this proposal," or "Jim, this plan is tailor-made just for you," or "Mary, you look beautiful! And you'll love this beautiful deal."

It isn't easy to always come on with *you*. It requires considerable effort and imagination. Sometime try writing a letter, especially a personal one, without a single use of I or me or my in it.

Common Poor Openers

Observe and you'll realize that most sales contracts open with either "whittlin' talk" about spouse, kids, golf or some personal reference in a phrase including I, me, or my.

"Mr. Williams, thank you for seeing *me*."
"Jack, *I* appreciate this opportunity."
"Mary, *I'm* happy to see you."

Eradicating the I, me, my and replacing it with *you* vastly improves the strength of your proposal and the prospects for an early closing. Primary factors in your presentation are the customer and the product you are selling.

The Elements of Closing the Sale

One could write a book on this—and probably in the process expand the phony mystique about closing. Appraising just the simple fundamentals keeps it concise and enhances more efficient application of your closing of sales.

1. Opening statement.
2. Proposal.
3. Benefits.
4. Objections, finding and disposing of.
5. Price opportunities.
6. Supply and demand.
7. Prospect attitude.

From the opening statement move as quickly as possible into the proposal. Often, as you well know, the prospect will attempt to divert you or soften you up with inconsequential conversation. Only your judgment can tell you how soon you can move from idle conversation to your proposal without seeming rude. Here are two ways to lessen this diversion. The best one is your prop. Placing your prop before the customer as you make your opening statement will usually preempt the casual conversation. The second way to lessen the diversion is the obvious one of not adding to it. If the customer wants to tell about the fish he or she caught, you listen. But don't tell about the one you caught—and especially not a bigger fish!

Knowing that there is an appropriate prop for every sales situation, and using it, enables you to get into your proposal and on to your closing.

Keep Your Closing Objective Primary and Moving

It may appear unfriendly, cold, and callous to even suggest eradicating the casual opening discussion. This soft-sell, old-style salesmanship is deeply ingrained and is almost a part of the lore. But it can be terribly inefficient. Whittlin' talk holds little value towards sharpening your winning edge in selling and rapidly expanding your income.

Your perspective and control of the situation makes a casual opening discussion an obsolete element of your selling. If your product is so dull that you'd rather talk about almost anything else, you've simply got to find a new product. Your objective is to sell your product, and there is nothing—absolutely nothing—more important, more exciting, and more interesting to talk about than your product and how it fits this prospect.

Making it exciting and interesting with your opening statement and the attention-getting prop will usually pleasingly preempt all of the weather, sports, and family chatter. Certainly you have been involved in those lengthy diversionary discussions that are finally interrupted with, "Well let's hear your pitch." The proposal was incidental to the conversation. Not very important. Why should anyone bother to buy it?

Making your product the most important thing of the moment is vital to closing. Using diamonds, gold, silver, coins, a knife, a balloon—whatever launches into your proposal—can be much more pertinent and provocative than any other conversation. You're guaranteed that it will assist in closing the sale faster. And it's not the least bit unfriendly or antisocial.

It reminds me of Herb M.'s traveling presentation with the "diamond" the size of a cantaloupe. It was placed on the center of the table, covered by a red velvet cloth. As Herb ceremoniously removed the cloth, all eyes were riveted on the huge "diamond." All of Herb's following quality sales points were supported by the concept of the quality of diamonds.

Diversionary Discussion Inhibits the Close

Real estate salesperson Patricia L. has her own very astutely conceived method of obliterating unessential discourse. On a single sheet of paper she has an attractively printed list of questions. These questions may sound like small talk but they all focus in on the customer profile as it relates to finding the right property for that prospect.

Patricia's salespeople are grilled on this list. They never show the list of questions to anyone, especially not to a prospect. It is carefully memorized. The attractive printing of the list may seem like a minor tactic; however, like Herb's diamond, the elegance of presentation is part of "selling the sales staff."

Strict adherence to this list is a proven means of getting to the sale more quickly through what appears to be the friendliest of conversations. It doesn't drift. It is efficient selling, leaving nothing in the preamble to chance. As mentioned earlier, Patricia L. sells far more real estate than any competitor in her territory.

2. THE OPENING CLOSE

Winning selling requires the use of those techniques that most often achieve a closing as early as possible in the presentation.

The Significance of Simplicity

Nick R. is a highly successful local advertising man, specializing in radio advertising. His method of selling is charmingly simple and boldy direct: He walks in on a prospect with almost an affront:

> "Mr. Jones, you should be using radio advertising."
> "Why?"
> "Because your sales will increase."
> "How do you know that?"
> "Through several of my customers whose sales are up very nicely."
> "Oh. What did they do?"
> "Something just like this." (Nick's prop is usually a sheet he has prepared using gold stars pasted on a program schedule to dramatize the spots he is proposing.)

Nick's opening line is a closing statement: "You should be using radio advertising." It sounds blunt, but it fits Nick. His simple technique demonstrates the efficiency of the opening close. It leads promptly to the basic benefit of increased sales and then to the selection process with the gold stars.

Radio can be very complex. There are books full of statistics. The research defining the audience of each station is detailed and highly professional. Nick knows his product and how to use the research. But the important reason for investing in radio—or any advertising—is to increase sales.

Nick earns commissions in excess of $50,000 annually in a market of about 60,000 people with his simple opening close system. The first line asks for an order.

Finding the Most Direct Line to the Order

Setting the stage quickly, efficiently, and with appropriate enticement leads directly into the proposal. Different types of products may require more detailed, or technical, support in the presentation. Nevertheless, every worthwhile product or service has a fundamental or primary need. Despite the research, the engineering, the cost—all the back-up data—getting to the basic need promptly in your proposal guarantees faster closings. There's no mystique to that. It's simple common sense, offering your product benefits such as:

- Lower costs
- Makes sales
- Increases productivity
- Adds attractiveness
- Makes the buyer look good
- Keeps you warm
- Tastes good

There's always one *most* compelling reason to buy. State that early and as often as you feel is appropriate. That one compelling reason is the most direct line to the order. It asks for the order. Also, there is always at least one, possibly a fast 1-2-3, statement of convincing proof of the benefit. The proof also asks for the order.

Incredible: "Did You Request the Order?"

Looking at this part of so-called professional selling skills from a very high-class company, is to me appalling. Winning selling doesn't beg the order. It states the customer-gains. The customer doesn't get those advantages without the order. For sure! It proffers the proof of the product's advantages. That proof urges the commitment.

If the benefit suffices, the proof is convincing, and the price is right, nod your head, "Okay?" If further objections stand in your way of the close, ferret them out and dispose of them. Then nod again, "All right?" You've been through it a thousand times. All I'm stressing here is getting to your close as quickly as possible—more quickly—because your time is money. Faster closing enables more calls in a day, more sales, and your rapidly growing income. We're talking money. Not theory. Every word you utter and every demonstration of evidence you make urges commitment.

My friend and long-time sales associate, Bill T., whom you've met before in this book, was a stickler for detail. When he prepared a presentation, the prospect was bound to sit still for the whole thing. Bill was thorough to a fault, but a dedicated, productive, and respected salesperson.

Once when Bill was on vacation, I covered for him on a major account that was in the process of buying in several markets. The buyer's name was John. He was persuaded to close several orders quickly based on the threat that otherwise he would be forced to receive Bill's full and meticulous presentations on his return. It became a joke in a way between John and myself.

> "John, buy it now or Bill's going to be here with fire in his eye."
> "I think I'll wait."
> "John, you're going to get the *full* pitch."
> "Well, I think . . ."
> "John, you know it's what you want."
> "Okay," John laughed, "but only to avoid that big pitch!"

You've often heard—and practiced, I'm sure—the admonition:

"When you close the sale, say thank you and leave promptly." It's a good sales basic. Less frequently heard is the suggestion to get the sale with the fewest amount of words, in the shortest span of time. That, too, is a basic.

When my company went into business with a group of raw-recruit salespeople, instructions were, "Make twenty calls a day and be back at five with orders." Any sales staff that knew better would have just laughed. About six calls a day was the norm. But our people didn't know any better. They ran fast, sold hard, made twenty or more calls, and returned proudly at five with orders. It was too simple and too effective to totally survive the debilitating methods of tradition. However, it's good to know that they actually do still run faster and sell harder. It's ingrained in *their* tradition.

Super Selling Sequencing

With proper sequencing of the ingredients of your proposal, you carry it only far enough to get approval. Then you say thank you, shake hands, and depart with your order. But let the sequencing get out of sync, and a long, confusing, and laborious presentation may leave you empty-handed and discouraged. You're unhappy with yourself because you knew that it came off poorly. We all have bad days occasionally.

Your *opening close* system is simple and direct and planned to avoid the time-wasting, unproductive presentations that ramble to a "Well, we'll think about it" conclusion. Your super selling sequencing goes only as far as is necessary to secure the affirmative "Yes." That's all. Therefore, in the first few elements of closing you sequence positive elements that present a minimum of controversial material. You keep it all very simple to avoid entangling, debatable, and delaying factors.

Looking at it from another angle, this closing approach is your very best insurance to get an early closing. Furthermore, it gets you into your proposal most efficiently. Chances are that you will still close your sale sooner than by any other touted means.

Here are seven sure steps to guarantee faster closings:

1. The brief opening Y-O-U statement.

2. The eye-catching prop.

3. The primary advantage. Pause here. Ask "Okay?" If that advantage—or benefit—is sufficiently compelling, you may have your close right then.

4. The strongest proof. Again wait a beat or two. The advantage plus the proof may elicit the question: "What's the cost?"

5. The Price. You answer the question, or anticipated question, avoiding terms such as "cost, buying, spending." Instead, use labels like "value and investment." Wait. Nod and ask "All right? Shall we deliver?"

6. The prospect evaluation. This is an underlying thread from the moment you enter the office. You are measuring the client's moods. This at times can be the most important key to your closing. You adjust to the prospect. For example, if the customer is in a skeptical mood, you should be prepared to welcome his or her list of objections and dispose of them in an unflustered fashion. Some buyers take it as part of their job to try to instill fluster in salespersons.

7. The supply and the demand. If your product is in short supply and high demand, forget the foregoing. Call the customer on the phone with, "Good morning, Joan. You've got two carloads, okay?" Tough close! But remember when you're in a monopoly position: ladle out the service and attention toward the day when competition returns.

3. THE POWERFUL SILVER PEN CLOSE

One of the secrets of winning selling is the use of appropriate gifts. It's a secret only because so few salespeople do it. This subject of gifts was discussed in chapter 8, but is retrieved here in a different connotation, as it relates to closing.

Verbal orders are common to many businesses. You can buy stocks, advertising, and much retail merchandise with just a phone call. Conversely, automobiles, insurance, real estate, and numerous other purchases require your name on the dotted line. One of our sales reps used to say, "Nothing is ever sold until it is sold properly." Part of the "properly" is a firm commitment. It's easy for a customer to squirm out of a verbal order with, "I changed my mind."

It's not our objective to try to convert the verbal order business and slow the sale process with some new form. If your business operates on verbal orders, there may still be many instances when your judgment tells you to add firmness to your close by means of getting the customer's signature on a confirmation.

People Do Like to Sign Their Names

There's an element of ego in a signature. It's a trademark for that individual. Except for clever forgery, that signature is an exclusive part of that person. It's a well-known sales angle to capitalize on the inclination of people to put their signature on the line. And of course, there are other shrewd operators who have a policy to "sign nothing."

Add to this the attractiveness of various writing instruments. At this moment within my vision are twenty-six pens— no, thirty-eight. My wife buys them by the boxful, and I just spotted an unopened box. When the President signs bills, he gives away pens used in the signing. There is a definite allure in pens. Some especially elegant ones are actually jewelry. Others appear ornate, but are really inexpensive giveaways.

My good friend, Ken M., is in the wholesale oil business. You may be sure that he never parts with a truckload of oil or gasoline without a name on the line. On my desk is a "silver" pen from Ken. When you're about to sign a deal with Ken, he offers his "silver" pen. It's part of his closing technique: "Here, sign it with my pen." Then he chuckles, "Keep it as a souvenir of one of your better deals." A color photo of Ken's always smiling face is on the end of the pen that points toward the writer.

Pens Are Closing Tools

It's a gracious and friendly gesture, when you sense the moment of acquiescence, to take the "silver" pen from your pocket and, with a smile of victory, to offer it to your prospect. "Jack, your famous autograph, please. And the pen is yours as a memento of this occasion." The combination of autograph-inclination and the offering of a gift helps to lubricate the closing process in those selling situations in which a signed commitment is required.

You've observed certain people with a shirt pocket holding a half-dozen pens and pencils. It illustrates the strange allure of writing instruments. Those scribblers are there not as gifts, but to be used for some essential purpose. Most of the salespersons I've known closely own a fine pen they flourish with pride. It not only writes with reliability, but also makes an attractive pointer for a presentation.

Your Unique Technique

With a technique so obvious as unusual pens for a gift, especially in association with a closing, it's surprising how seldom it is applied. The President of the U.S. gives bill-signing pens. Plastic advertising pens abound. Other than my friend, Ken M., I don't know of anyone using this "silver" pen technique. It's probably wide open for your exclusive benefit. Your closings will gain an extra aura of charm. Your individual trademark will be enhanced. More sales and faster closings will be yours.

The Ultimate Silver Pen Closer

For a period of time, my desk in New York City was graced with an elegant silver pen standing in a beautiful silver stand. My wife had found it at an antique auction. Its dollar value wasn't as high as it would appear from its attractiveness. Whenever some new acquaintance entered my office, that pen always caught their eye and elicited comment.

An occasion finally arose in which my beautiful silver pen was elected to be a sacrifice to a sale. We had lost an exclusive client in Miami and were determined to get him back. Frank B. pointed at my lovely pen. "Use it." Sadly I concurred.

We planned a group presentation in a private club dining room. Five of us were meeting with two of them. Each of us had specific subjects to cover. We were well rehearsed. The pen was our silent partner.

When Bob and Ralph, our sales targets, arrived at our meeting room, my silver pen was in the center of the table, hidden from view under a black velvet cloth. Bob instantly asked, "Hey, what's that?"

Attempting to give our prop an aura of suspense, Frank said, "You'll learn soon enough, but first . . ."

"Will it explode?" Bob asked in wide-eyed jest.

With every point we attempted to make, Bob interrupted with, "Hey, what's that?" gesturing at the pen.

Finally in feigned exasperation, Frank yanked the black velvet off of the beautiful pen and holder. "It's yours, Robert. Yours to keep forever *after* you sign this document." Frank placed the elegant pen and the contract in front of Bob.

Bob and Ralph examined the trophy with appropriate appreciation. Bob said, "Can't I have it anyway—even if I don't sign this?"

Frank wagged his head, "Never."

"Maybe," Ralph interposed laughing, "the pen's worth more than any business they might get us."

I'd like to be able to tell you that Bob signed then and there. He didn't. But he did depart with my pen. And some positive assurances. The contract was signed that week. Our carefully planned and rehearsed presentation never fully came off. The silver pen was the pitch. It served its purpose.

4. CREATIVE CLOSING THAT WINS FOR YOU

Your single most important, and inviolable, rule of closing is: Never leave it to chance. Much selling does just that. It's expected, or hoped for, or prayed for, but not adequately planned for. That is probably why so much mystique surrounds the close. A barrage of words, facts, claims, proof, support data, prices, and so on, are thrown at a prospect. At some point he or she buys. Then the salesperson may wonder what it was that closed the sale.

My "Gotta Guys" didn't receive an adequate amount of advance training. There wasn't enough time. The simple strategy was to make more calls than any competitor—just to be there, early and often, and to keep your transom open. Joe was a super salesperson, loaded with natural talent, a marvelous personality, and a hunger for success. He also had a strong curiosity.

"A funny thing happened today," Joe said at the end of his twenty-call day. "There's this nice guy—always sees me—that I've called on for two weeks trying to get an order for St. Louis. This morning he gave me an order." Joe laughed. "It surprised me. I said thanks, grabbed the order, and ran."

Joe paused to light a cigarette. "After lunch," he continued, "curiosity got the best of me. I went back to see him to try to find out what it was that I had said or shown him that had closed the sale. He said, 'Oh, nothing. It was just that you were here so often.'" Persistence. Not exactly a shrewd closing technique. It does get orders, though. Shotgun fashion.

Imagination, the Key to Creative Closing

Relieving me of my cherished silver pen as a prop to get our Miami client back in the fold was a product of Frank's imagination. It was a thing that effectively fit that specific selling situation.

All efficient and faster closings emerge from a plan. Knowing your customer enables you to more accurately plan:

1. The Y-O-U opening
2. The prop
3. The primary advantage
4. The clinching proof
5. The attractive price (all prices are "attractive")

This is *careful* planning. Too often a salesperson depends on a "great personal relationship" and doesn't plan adequately. Later he or she is bewildered that their great friend bought the competition. It would have been wise to have thought in advance that the "great personal relationship" *especially* deserved an extra amount of imaginative planning.

Cold prospecting or cold selling, for example, when the prospect walks into an automobile showroom, requires a fast-on-the feet reaction. "May I help you?" is a terrible opening cliché. Furthermore, the *I* precedes the *you*! Lint-picking? Well it's the little things that often make the big difference. What's wrong with, "Good morning! You're looking for a new automobile. There's bound to be a beauty here for you. What's your name?"

Any competent automobile salesperson should have several well-planned Y-O-U openers memorized and on the tip of his or her tongue. The sales manager should assist the effort and also devise a couple of appropriate props to help the close. The Y-O-U opening and certain appropriate props (such as Allan's tie clasp and Ken's pen) will help firm up the wobbly price.

Cold Prospecting Needs a Warm Opening

Your opening is slanted somewhat differently in cold prospecting. You must be especially careful that it doesn't have a smart-alec, a presumptive, or a challenging ring to it. And you don't want to be apologetic for breaking in on the customer. When we were kids in high school, some of us earned our money simonizing cars on the weekends. During the week, in the early evenings, we did our soliciting. Out of the mouth of babes came the simple, direct Y-O-U opener: "Good evening, sir, would *you* be interested in having *your* car simonized?"

"Good morning, Miss Smithers, would *you* be interested in executive stationery which could save *your* company as much as $25,000 a year?" It's simple, direct, and identifies the product and a strong benefit in one sentence. You can think of several other common openings with I, me, my product, and so on: "I'd appreciate a few moments to tell you . . ." or "May I show you . . ." or "I have something which should interest you and save you. . ."

Imagination Always Finds the Creative Closing Elements

Funny thing about imagination—it always works. It will never let you down. There exists a huge bank of knowledge, ideas, things, techniques, and experience inside of your mental computer. By putting this computer to work to come up with creative elements for a specific closing situation, it will respond.

It may take a little time for your imagination to produce the best choices.

Ask your computer the following questions:

- What single factor is most appealing to this prospect?
- What can I do to dramatize my product's fit to that appeal factor?
- What objections are likely to be raised?
- What are the simplest answers to each objection?
- What is the most convincing proof to buy?

This is a kind of brainstorming. Jot down everything that comes to mind. The process of elimination filters out the best answers to your questions. These answers readily form your new creative closing system that wins for you.

Keeping It Simple Is Creative

Like the simple lines of a masterpiece work of art, your adherence to the foregoing simple closing plan is a source of continuing satisfaction. By planning creatively for your closing of the sale, you eliminate numerous elements which tend only to delay the close.

Sometimes Leverage Speeds a Closing

The factor of leverage was left out of our plan because most often the presence of a leverage element is happenstance. If it's there, you use it. If it's not there, creating leverage comes out devious and antiproductive. Obviously, if you sell home appliances, and a car dealer is looking at your appliances, and you are in need of a new truck, you have some leverage working. So does the dealer. This reciprocity could be the closing element for both of you.

Occasionally you run into an incredible leverage situation. One in my experience was with a radio station in Seattle. The city's principal drug wholesaler had held back on reordering certain popular products until the manager of the station was about to make a sales trip to New York. The drug wholesaler gave his friend the station manager a pocketful of product orders—each of which required a supporting radio advertising order on the station. That was leverage! Our client, the station manager, would never reveal how he worked his deal with the drug wholesaler.

There is nothing more important to the winning edge in selling than a strong closing technique. Obviously it's your big money-maker. Securing a higher percentage of closings and getting them faster will make your income soar to substantially higher levels. The simple seven-step plan will keep you on the beam and prevent your falling into the common error of leaving the closing to chance. Without the close, the preliminary sales investment is a loss. We're interested only in wins. Use this new creative system with confidence and you'll win a bundle of new dollars in your income.

Summary

These are your daily dozen successful techniques for closing more frequently and faster:

    I. Develop the Y-O-U opening line.

    II. Use a prop to divert inconsequential conversation.

    III. Know that the most interesting and exciting conversation is about your product.

    IV. Apply the simple and direct opening close.

    V. Stress the single most potent customer-gain from acquiring your product.

    VI. Make your every element ask for a commitment.

    VII. Work your seven simple steps to guaranteed faster closings.

VIII Use the "silver pen" as a closing tool.

    IX. Plan your simple creative closing system. Never leave it to chance.

    X. Modify your cold-prospecting approaches.

    XI. Define key creative closing factors with your imagination.

    XII. Mold these points wrung from your imagination into your strong new creative closing system.

A FINAL WORD

You know it. It's I-M-P-R-O-V-E-M-E-N-T. The higher your attainment, the more you seek other successful techniques.

It's infinite. The total scope of professional selling is limitless, there's always more to be learned. That's a large part of the excitement, of the enthusiasm, of the dedication.

In my sales company we bought every appealing book on selling for each of our salespersons. They read them eagerly, discovered and applied new ideas. Their sales volume and their incomes increased dramatically.

To me the nuances in selling described in this book offer the greatest opportunity for professional growth. Expanding imagination, using the idea opener, working the studied negative, applying the six-way voice instrument, building better language and literally hundreds of other often overlooked subtleties . . . each adds a percentage point of IMPROVEMENT.

Develop your nuances of the winning edge. No matter how competent you are now, you will grow 100% to your amazement in your thrill of achievement and in your increased income.

I won't wish you luck. There's no need to, you already have it. In abundance!

Robert E. Eastman

INDEX